Rebell

Carausius and Allectus

The Welshmen who stole the Roman Empire

John Pitts

First published in Great Britain 2022

© John Pitts, 2022
John Pitts has asserted his right under the Copyright, Designs and Patents Act, 1988, to be identified as Author of this work.

This is a work of fiction. All characters, apart from the obvious historical figures in this book are fictitious and any resemblance to actual persons, living or dead, is entirely coincidental.

All rights reserved. No part of this publication may be reproduced or transmitted in any form or by any means, electronic or mechanical, including photocopying, recording, or any information storage or retrieval system, without prior permission in writing from the Author.
johnpitts49@icloud.com

No responsibility for loss caused to any individual or organization acting on or refraining from action as a result of the material in this publication can be accepted by the author.

British Library Cataloguing-in-Publication Data

A catalogue record for this book is available from the British Library.
ISBN: 978-1-3999-3287-5

To Yvonne, whose family history
led to my uncovering of this
piece of British history.

Background

The Roman empire in the third century was beset with problems of revolts in many areas. Controlling and governing an area of its size was proving difficult and expensive. An era of delegation and devolution was instituted by Diocletian, who was the Roman emperor from AD284 to 305. Born to a family of low status in the Roman province of Dalmatia, Diocletian rose through the ranks of the military to become cavalry commander to the Emperor Carus. After the deaths of Carus and his son Numerian on campaign in Persia, Diocletian was proclaimed emperor after defeating the other son of Carus, the debauched Carinus. Diocletian's reign stabilized the empire, and marked the end of the Crisis of the Third Century. He appointed fellow officer, Maximian, as Caesar in AD285 and promoted him further as Augustus, co-emperor, in AD286.

Diocletian delegated further in AD293, appointing Galerius and Constantius as caesars, junior co-emperors. Under this 'tetrarchy,' or 'rule of four,' each emperor would rule over a quarter-division of the empire. Diocletian further secured the empire's borders and purged it of all threats to his power. Maximian was made emperor of the Western Roman Empire, and this area included the island of Britain. He had campaigned in Gaul for much of his career, and through this he met a young Welshman, sent to him to serve Rome as a way of securing his father's loyalty. After demonstrating bravery and leadership he was allowed to return to his family, only to be called on again when Maximian faced a different sort of problem. Things did not quite work out as he wished.

List of characters

AINE Wife of Caradog, ruler of Dyfed

ALBINUS Military trainer, army of Maximian

ALLECTUS/XANDER Son of Arthfael of Siluria

ALYS Older daughter of Ceris/Carausius

ANWEN Girlfriend and wife of Ceris/Carausius

ARTHFAEL Half-brother of Caradog

ASCLEPIODOTUS Praetorian Prefect, deputy to Constantius

BRONWEN Younger daughter of Ceris/Carausius

BRYCHAN Son of Caradog, older brother of Ceris/Carausius

CARADOG, ruler of Dyfed, father of Ceris/Carausius

CARAUSIUS/CERIS Younger son of Caradog of Dyfed

CERIS/CARAUSIUS Younger son of Caradog of Dyfed

CHRESIMA Grecian slave girl to family of Flavius Valentinus

CONSTANTIUS Military commander, junior emperor of Rome

DARIUS Slave from Mesopotamia

DECIMUS Military comrade of Ceris/Carausius

DIOCLETIAN , Military commander, later Emperor of the Roman Empire

DOMNALL Pictish leader in Caledonia

FLAVIUS VALENTINUS Financial administrator for the empire in London

FULVIUS PAULINUS Roman governor of Britain

GAIUS IULIUS MARCELLUS Naval commander, port of Dover

GRIFUD Son of Caradog, older brother of Ceris/Carausius

LIVIA Wife of Flavius Valentinus

LLYR Old shipwright in Wales

MARCUS Son of Flavius

MAXIMIAN Military general, later Caesar and Augustus, emperor of Western Roman empire

PROBINUS Army commander, Tertius' deputy

QUINTUS Army commander, Maximian's envoy to Britain

TERTIUS Senior army commander in Britain

XANDER/ALLECTUS Son of Arthfael, ruler of Siluria

Chapter 1

Caradog

'Bloody Romans,' muttered Caradog, as he left his hall, the place from which his ancestors had ruled too. Arguing with himself, he had to concede that they mostly left him alone if he gave them what they thought due, and ruling with their permission, he had maintained his power. Indeed his wealth had grown and his people thrived along with this. Prosperous in our subservience, he thought.

The Welsh had been defeated by the invading Roman army two hundred years earlier, and now in these lands of south-west Wales they managed to exist together in peaceful stability while both benefited through trade. Conquered first by his ancestors from Ireland, the land was then lost to the Romans as after mighty resistance and bloodshed, defeat had been accepted after the valiant stand of Caratacus in the great mountains of the north. Rather than rule directly over a resentful population, the Romans wisely left the existing ruling families in place. That they had to behave, pay taxes and tributes of course was reluctantly accepted by the Welsh, and in complying some rulers had recognised and even adopted some of the habits of the Romans.

The people of this corner of Wales sailed the seas in their ships taking goods this way and that, from Wales to Ireland and mainland Europe. Rich in metals and fertile for growing crops and raising sheep and cattle, this was a good land. Minerals, wool, wood, grain or even sheep, bringing back oils, fabrics and wines, it all brought profits to the ruling family. On this fine day, the air was fresh, and the sky was clear with a few fronds of high cloud tainting an otherwise blue expanse. The sea in the distance reflected that blueness, broken only by the occasional wavelet. Around the town dark rocky outcrops raised their heads among the vivid green of the fields where flocks of sheep grazed contentedly.

The white flag with the red dragon flew proudly over the great hall of Caradog, king of that part of Wales called Dyfed. It stood overlooking the town and its harbour on a high rocky promontory. The area of the hall was in the grounds of an old hill fort from the days before the Romans were even thought of. The remains of earthen ramparts surrounded his hall and with the outer ditch they still looked steep. With his three brothers, they ruled over the entirety of Wales but this part was his alone. He had adopted the dragon as his symbol. A mythical fire-breathing beast, equipped with great claws and considered invincible, it represented the monster of one's dreams, the one that children use to frighten themselves late at night, in the way that children have always invented something greater than themselves in a mystical world. It is said that it came from the Romans, who carried dragon-shaped hollow devices on poles that made wailing noises with the wind as they went into battle against savages. A long way from breathing fire, Caradog had thought, but the image of the imaginary beast sometimes twisted and snapped in the wind and almost appeared to take on a life of its own. He was a fine looking man, approaching half a century on this earth, whose height and general appearance together with his confident manner gave him an aura of kingship and he was respected by his people in turn. His actions brought them safety and security and he was known to adjudicate fairly in disputes laid before him.

It wasn't the flag he looked at this time as he left the hall, though, distracted as he was by his thoughts. He usually couldn't ignore the sense of pride he got from admiring this symbol of his power but his brow furrowed as he strode into the town where he had a meeting with his brother Arthfael. They were not alike and indeed had different mothers. Arthfael was the ruler of neighbouring Siluria, the eastern part of southern Wales. His land included the massive Roman fort at Caerleon where the Second Augusta Legion was based, and this was a permanent reminder to him that his position as ruler was dependent on others. Caradog wanted to meet him somewhere away from his hall as the presence of Arthfael dampened any good spirits. He was continually resentful of the occupation and hated Romans with a passion, and because of this had none of the friendly working relationships that Caradog had built up.

The whole town was preparing to celebrate the May festival. Bonfires were prepared on the town's green and houses proudly decorated with hawthorn flowers and branches, there was a stage for the fiddlers and already barrels of mead and ale stood ready for the celebrations of joy and fertility. A lot of sore heads tomorrow, he thought, and smiled at the thought of his people having some much deserved recreation. That evening the two royal families were meeting together in the hall for a private celebration of their own at this end of winter and start of spring but before that he and his family would walk among the crowds to show that they were part of this community. He also wanted to remind the people of his benevolence in paying most of the expenses, although he did not begrudge any of it.

He had arranged to meet Arthfael down at the harbour, which was a quiet place now the workers would be preparing for the celebrations. He wanted to clear the air of the latest grumbles, so both families could relax and enjoy it. Caradog thought he would give him the chance to vent any current feelings as that seemed to ease any tensions and give Arthfael some relief. Knowing his half-brother well, he realised that just letting him complain made him feel better as he got things off his chest. He also realised that little he could say would make much difference because it was in cooperating that good relationships developed. The Romans in his lands were as far away from their rulers as they could be, and relationships with the local people kept them happier. Caradog was aware of some relationships that developed with local women that were more than just friendships, and the families that formed, despite some difficulties in acceptance by some townsfolk, became more rooted to his lands.

He walked down through the town, and admired the improvements that prosperity had bought. Streets had been broadened and straightened in the Roman style. Many of the old round thatched buildings were being reconstructed in stone. He paid the taxes required of him without a grumble or a quibble and sent a few men as soldiers when it is demanded of him. Death and taxes, both inescapable, he thought. Thank the heavens the Romans can't tax a beautiful day. He reflected that his family for generations had lived with the sea, making profits through his fleet of trading vessels. Business was good. He had a fine wife and three fine sons who also took to the sea, and he saw no end to his line. As he walked, though, he couldn't help wondering if he was selling out to the Romans. They have brought us much, he was forced to concede, and we have new industries now. We have the quarries that provide the stones for building, we have stonemasons, lime kilns and the builders themselves. The Romans that now live here are making offices to service their forts and roads at the end of our high street towards the harbour. They are building villas over the hill where there is a spring to supply the baths of which they are so keen. Our fishermen and farmers keep them and the townsfolk well-supplied. Fresh fish are landed daily and sold from the quay and farmers sell their seasonal produce in the market square twice weekly. In the past, seasonal fevers and plagues have taken many lives, but drainage channels have reduced the smells that used to assault the noses of the town, and an apothecary has set up shop to provide remedies for the common complaints.

Will the Romans be here forever? If ever there was an uprising, there are five thousand troops at Caerleon. My people would die, and for what? Besides which, most of us are gaining. My ships travel ever more, bringing in what they want. Fine crockery and fabrics sell well. When the sheep are sheared the womens' workshops get busy with their spinning and weaving. The world is moving on and we must move too. He noticed how the fronts of two of the larger merchants had been replaced with marble and pillars and the Roman style of clothing that is being adopted more widely. We had lived with the Romans for generations before, with discipline and punishment as the watchword for us both. Now the balance is changing, they eat at my land with their quarries, and I fear becoming a king without power. He shrugged off the negative thoughts. Perhaps it is all for the best, he reflected.

He made his way to the harbour where Arthfael arrived on a great horse and dismounted with a grunt. As always he was dressed in dark clothing which complemented his scowling expression, which was not helped by his heavy features. His brows hung over his dark eyes, making them appear sunken and the skin of his face was coarse.

'How are things with you?' asked Caradog cheerfully, trying to lift his mood.

'Much the same' he replied, 'those Romans still take their taxes and buy food and materials before we have a chance to. I can't stand them. They think they own the place.'

'Well,' said Caradog 'When you think about it they do, but if you work with them rather than against them it can work well. We do good business and they use our ships to move their goods.'

As expected he started to grumble. 'That's all very well, but you don't have a legion sitting on your land. I can't fart without a Roman hearing it.'

Caradog laughed. 'There are some benefits, aren't there?' After a moment he decided to paint a rosier picture for him. ' Look at the road between our lands. You must admit it's easier riding now and your wife's carriage would struggle without it.' He thought for a minute. 'It's strange how they name their roads after women. They call our road Via Julia and the great road to the north is named after a Helen.' He hesitated and added 'Perhaps they just like walking over their women.'

Arthfael snorted 'They should try that with some of ours.'

Having got the conversation going, Caradog carried on,

'Arthfael, I am worried about your moods. As your older brother, I am expressing my concern. We are alive, at peace and have a strong family. What is really ailing you?'

Arthfael, not one to talk much, let alone confide in anyone, went quiet. Caradog allowed the silence until Arthfael said 'I think I'm unhappy because I see what you have and realise I am not as blessed. You have three fine sons to work with you and succeed you. I have Xander who is not like them.'

Caradog realised that Arthfael would have wanted a strapping warrior son for his heir, and that Xander was more reserved. He sometimes had to work for his father's attention, and when criticised, which was often, retreated into a sullen silence.

'You are hard on him. He is not yet a man and you expect him to act like one. When he is grown he will find his way and you have to accept that it may not be yours.'

Arthfael conceded with a small smile. 'You are wise, brother, I will try to look up to you without envy.'

Caradog replied 'Let's go to the hall and prepare our celebrations. It's a new year and we must look forwards.'

His great hall was built in the traditional way. Under a roof of thatch, supported by thick walls of rough stone was the meeting and entertaining area where townsfolk would expect him to adjudicate in disputes and he would hold great feasts of celebration. The floor was made of great stone slabs, strewn with rushes for freshness. The walls were whitewashed for brightness, stained only by the atmosphere of smokiness from the great fireplace in the centre. The smoke escaped through a hole in the roof but breezes often caused the plume to swirl around inside. After many generations of use, the timbers inside were darkly stained. Behind the area were the quarters where he and his wife resided and the attached buildings at the sides were for his sons. Around the buildings ran a defensive wall of stone; there were no guards and the gates were always open as no dangers existed. Some barns and stables completed his estate and many servants tended to the family's needs. While this had been his home, and his predecessors before him, he couldn't help but compare this with the villas that the Romans were building. They built in stone, with tiled floors and painted plaster on the walls, and a courtyard in which to walk and converse. Their workmen cut the stones, baked the clay for the roof and floor tiles, and taught my people these skills. And what was most astonishing was how the Romans attended to their comfort. There were baths inside which were for relaxing, not just for a quick wash. Their floors were built of large clay tiles on pillars, and the space underneath was fed from a fire outside the building which made the floor itself warm When he was invited to see one, although in kindness and respect, he could not help feeling that these homes were so far of the future that he left with a feeling of dismay. Perhaps I am of the past and not the future.

In the afternoon, the two families started to gather. Arthfael's son Xander arrived with his mother. He had ridden alongside the carriage which clattered along on its iron edged spoked wheels. and he handed the reins of his horse to the driver to feed, water and stable. Xander was sixteen years old, slim of frame with a narrow face and the look of a wandering mystic or the monks who travel the country promoting a new religion from the east. He was thereby rather over-shadowed by Brychan and Grifud, the older sons of Caradog who were fully grown, confident, exuded strength and spoke their minds. They often spoke over him and he felt that he may as well not be there. He was familiar with his father's moods and tried to overcome his resentment of his cousins as he did not want to be regarded in the way that he knows his father can be. He tried to look attentive to the conversation and still joined in when he could although he knew that his views and opinions were limited through his lack of years. He quietly absorbed much of what was said to build his knowledge of the world in which they lived. Of the brothers, Ceris, the youngest, was closest to my age so he ought to be a natural friend, he thought. He too was very mature in his manner. I have seen his girlfriend too – a vision of beauty who made my body stir. I had to accept she wouldn't look at me, even considering the fact that I am probably just too young.

While it's good to get away from my father's court, where I am alone, he thought, I am resentful of these cousins, whose father trusts them, and allows them freedom while to mine I was a disappointment. I knew this, he couldn't hide it. It's in the way he looks at and speaks to me. Why couldn't he just love me for who I am? Ceris does speak to me, he is kind that way and has a way of behaving that does not put me down or treat me like a young fool who has not reached adulthood. But despite this, I was jealous of him; his looks and his girlfriend, and although he will never become king he was confident in his life. He was all the things I was not.

As they prepared to take refreshments, Caradog's wife Aine stood to take charge. She was famously forthright so everyone naturally deferred to her as she outlined the plans for the celebrations. She was determined to bring the families as close together as possible for the occasion. She called for the servants to bring drinks and food, and as she took a seat alongside two of her sons, she suddenly asked 'Where's Ceris?'

Grifud replied, 'I don't know, I haven't seen him all day.'

Brychan added 'He's probably down at the boat yard. I think he lives there.'

Grifud said 'He's often with that girl, the pretty one from the market'.

'I hope she's not leading him astray,' interjected Aine.

Grifud pretended to look shocked and teased his mother. 'I'm not sure who's doing the leading.'

She scowled and told one of them to go and find him. They looked at each other and shrugged. 'Hurry, we must go to the town before we start our own celebrations. One of you, just go as I tell you.'

Chapter 2

Quintus

I have been summoned to my general Maximian, busily campaigning in the depths of Gaul. so I am proceeding as fast as I can to find his headquarters. He lives as luxuriously as possible in his large canvas tent, which for a campaigning general is about as good as it gets. He is through and through a warrior, a fighting man, with little regard for the niceties of politeness. He is not a man to cross. He claims to serve Rome, of course, but his first loyalty is to himself. I cannot know what he wants of me. I can't think of anything I have done or not done that would merit his displeasure, but you never really know. I am known as a hard man and I have had to be to get where I am. He is a big man; burly, bearded and usually bad-tempered. He bears scars from old wars and has studied tactics of many battles. Now older he stays behind the lines but controls the action closely. I have served him for years in the Roman army. I have killed for him and taken wounds. He knows that I was lowly born and that everything I have I have earned for myself. He also knows he has the power to take it away. I have seen his brutality. He shows no mercy to the barbarians he captures or the soldiers who fail him.

It is said he came from lowly origins too, as does his old military comrade, Diocletian. I thought before I knew him that it might make him sympathetic to my situation, but having made it to the top of the army himself he does not want anyone else to follow. I suspect those two young generals have plans for the future. Having connections is all very well if you are ambitious, but it doesn't pay to get too close to an emperor as you rise in importance. In my time I have served under several and managed to keep my distance. What a position! I don't know why people want to become emperors. Their reigns are usually short, and have violent ends, either from a disillusioned army general or their own families! They say that power corrupts but it is also true that power makes jealousy in those who desire it and do not have it.

'Quintus Aurelius Silvanus, my old friend, you have come at good speed' says Maximian, lounging on a sofa. 'Sit and take some wine.' He seems uncommonly relaxed, and that makes me suspicious. 'You have served Rome well and you have impressed me with your manner and efficiency over many years. I need men like you in my service, proper men.'

I note the words 'my service' and wonder what is coming next. 'Yes, I feel you are destined for a higher rank,' he says thoughtfully 'Military success can lead to a political career as well as breeding.'

I feel more hopeful that something good will come of this but my suspicion remains lurking in the background.

'For your career, with my support, you need a new challenge, one which will teach you greater skills and also offer you the chance to become wealthier. A man needs money behind him in this world.'

I don't know if that is meant to worry me or appeal to me. Certainly now I have little to my name apart from the reputation I have built serving him. He lifts a codicil of appointment from the table beside him and waves it casually in my direction.

'I am making you my envoy to the island of Britain. The present governor is failing to deliver the taxes and tribute and this needs rectifying soon. I know he was appointed by the senate and ranks above me, but sometimes they send the less-favoured as far away as possible. As the nearest and most senior general I am held responsible for all this and have to sort out any messes that may happen.'

He looks at me, seeking my reaction. I keep my face blank, then say 'I am honoured that you should choose me, but I know little of that island other than its position at the very edge of the empire. Are you sure I am the right man for this?'

Maximian's face clouds and I fear a return to his usual state of mind. 'What I am sure of is that you have the right qualities and in my opinion that makes you the best man for this appointment. I don't need another bloody diplomat' he said pointedly, 'just a few years and after that you will return to my service here or in Rome itself.'

He hands me the codicil of appointment and as I take it he says 'Take ship from Boulogne, report to the governor in London and give him this. He is to return to me here. I am giving you a detachment of a dozen legionaries as an escort. The British tribes are generally pacified and accepting of their situation. Leaders that comply are left in position, and punishment for resistance must be harsh, and they know it.'

I salute and leave his headquarters. This was not what I expected. To serve for years on an island of wild but conquered tribes feels more like a punishment that I do not deserve. I found the harbourmaster and arranged transport for myself and my escort on the next available transport. I learned quickly that I was not a sailor. The small ship crashed through the waves in the great channel and I could see that the rowers struggled to keep coordination. As the ship lurched and twisted, my stomach wanted to empty and I started to sweat. Looking around, some of my escort obviously felt the same. I could not imagine anyone getting used to this. It was a relief to make dry land at the port of Dover. We spent the night at the castle recovering and the next day we were provided with horses. After three days we reached the walls of the city of London.

Arriving at the governor's palace was a surprise. It was not as primitive as I expected and the palace was a fine stone building. As I was shown in, I walked on fine tiled floors representing scenes of gods and strange animals. The walls were decorated too, and I felt that I could have been in one of our capital cities on the mainland. My spirits lifted as I talked with Fulvius Paulinus, the current governor. He was elderly and running to fat and I could see that he was dependent on others to fulfil his duties. I doubted if he had been outside London for years, and as no horse could carry him he would have to travel slowly in a carriage. He was affable enough and explained what was necessary in his role. I gently asked why Maximian had said he was failing to collect Rome's dues.

'It's not as easy as you think. First, there are many tribes to collect from. I try to set a realistic amount to demand. The south of the island is rich in producing grain and we trade at a fair price. Harvests can fail and I understand that. Maximian expects a regular amount as he is unwilling to accept a reality that he can't control. The west of the island is rich in minerals including gold, but mines collapse and seams run out. The poor people work with the simplest of hand tools too.'

'You seem to have some sympathy for these people, perhaps too much,' I say.

'I have got to know many. They are people like us, with dreams and ambitions and living under the yoke of Rome takes away their pride. I just try to treat them fairly, and to that end there has not been a major rebellion for years.'

'What will you do now?' I asked.

He replied 'I wish it was time for me to retire. That must be near. I have a farm outside Rome and I long to return there. I can have a quiet life in the countryside away from unpleasant tyrants and incessant demands. You will do well to follow my advice about being reasonable and fair. If you can keep Maximian at arm's length all the better. He doesn't seem to understand the reality of life here. Send him reports and keep them short and positive. With luck his thoughts will move on to some other poor soul.'

I reflected on his thoughts as I arranged to have my

belongings moved in. Perhaps he had become too kind. I tried to remember how long he had been here. Being away from scrutiny can make a man lax. I realised that he did not have much fear of Maximian and wondered if he had ever met him. That would account for his apparent nonchalance, and he tensed when I told him that Maximian had summoned him.

I set up quarters for my escort and left them to familiarize themselves with London. No doubt they will soon find the fleshpots, I thought. I warned them that we would soon be travelling around inspecting my new areas and to enjoy themselves while they could. In the meantime I pored over the records and ledgers until I had a headache. This is not for me, I thought, I am too much a soldier.

After leaving it as long as I could, I made my farewells to Paulinus and we set off on our tour of the lands. Several of my soldiers had become ill, and a couple had been injured in brawls. I concluded that this proved that they had enjoyed themselves. I bought the best horses on the market and set off with six of my soldiers as my escort. We looked strong enough and there had been no reports of disturbances. With our polished uniforms and visible weaponry I thought we would be safe enough. We travelled mostly on well-made roads planned by our engineers and built by our legions. I mused on how much we had put into these islands. The profits of trade must make it worth it. I realised now why it was important that trade and taxes continue to work to our benefit.

So many tribes! We called on the rulers of so many; Catuvellauni, Trinovantes, the Iceni whose Boudicca caused us trouble for a while, and many more. I introduced myself to those in power and explained my purpose of ensuring that they contributed on time what Rome demanded. I did not make any changes there and then, remembering Paulinus's advice. I had appointed my most educated soldier as record-keeper, and everything about the status quo was written down. My bearing as a senior military officer was enough to promote my authority and there was generally an air of acceptance. I did not hold a rank above Paulinus, of course, as he was appointed by the senate but would not be reluctant to express my opinions. We military people did not hold much brief for those wet-behind-the-ears types awarded governorships as rewards. They need us to hold things together if things get ugly.

The thing that struck me, having fought against many primitive but fierce people, was the similarity of the peasant folk, who lived a basic life in their round houses of wood and thatch, and the variation among their rulers, who had their fine halls but some seemed to have adopted some of the ways of Rome. Some tribes had leadership structures that seemed organised, with towns that were doing well. The further away we got from London, the less of our influence I could see, and for many there was obviously no love lost for Rome. All this I noted and dictated to my appointed scribe. We stayed in the many small Roman forts rather than accept any accommodation offered, though. I was a soldier in my heart and I enjoyed the company of rough brave men with stories to tell. After several months we had seen and examined England.

It was now time to go to the area in the west known as Wales. I knew there were tribes we called the Demetae and

Ordovices and the one called the Silures where we had our legion based in the fort at Caerleon, where we stayed for a few days to rest the horses. Off we travelled to meet them on our fine network of roads, joining the small forts which gave us hospitality and lodgings. We rode along the coast through Siluria where huge corrugations of hills and valleys descended to the sea, meeting an expanse of sand dunes and beaches. As we travelled further west to the land of the Demetae I was struck by the changes in the scenery. The sun was shining, the land was green and fertile, sheep grazed in the meadows and on the hillsides and crops were planted and growing to maturity. The rocks of the mountain tops were rugged and dramatic, and their darkness contrasted with the green of the fields and pastures. The long golden sandy beaches were like nothing I had ever seen before and I watched the gentle rhythm of wave after wave reach the shoreline in a lazy procession. I enjoyed riding and had spent much time in the saddle, so the travelling did not feel a chore. Maximian felt a world away for now as I watched this changing world and went to meet the inhabitants of the lands of the Demetae of Dyfed.

Chapter 3

Llyr

I don't know my age. I know that I am old because I see it from my hands. Between the scars is skin that has thinned, and if I see my reflection my face looks like a walnut shell. My bones ache and my joints creak, but I still manage to get my work done. My family has served the family of Caradog for generations. They are traders and I run the shipyard and harbour. Pride does not become an ordinary man, but when I look at the ships I have built and looked after, I do feel it inside. I see their lines, smell the timbers and know that they are as good as any others. I choose the woods, the pine, ash, oak and spruces. I have the stickiness of resins on my skin and the burns from the pitch we use to seal the hulls. I keep my workmen busy, and revel in the sounds of construction and creation as ships are born. The sounds of sawing and hammering echo around the harbour, and I see the smoke from the forge where my smiths make nails, rings and the tools that we use. I learned my skills from my father, and he from his father before. Sadly I have no son, he and my wife died with a fever ten years ago, but I have passed my skills to my workmen. The best of them will follow me when I am no longer able.

I was named after Llyr Llediarth, who founded the line of Caradog so long ago. He came from a settlement in Ireland where the Menapians traded and made a town. That poor tribe that came from the low countries was attacked by savage Germanic tribes and suffered greatly when a great flood devastated the marshy lands that gave them protection and sanctuary. They were subject to the great forces of nature, and by all accounts used to living with them until another force of nature arrived to threaten them. That force was called Julius Caesar and against his army they put up fierce resistance at the beginning. Many were killed and some fled to join their trading settlements around the coasts.

Llyr's descendents did well, coming to rule these lands, despite the presence of the Romans, and having rebelled against them in the past. Great king Einudd had four sons who between them now rule all of Wales. His eldest, Caradog, is a fine and fair ruler. He uses his wealth wisely. While some kings store and hide their treasures, he spends much of his on his towns and people. He understands the Romans. If he cooperates they leave him pretty well alone. His three brothers in the other lands are less accepting of Roman rule. Caradog I think uses the Romans as they use him. Our town has changed with these times. The great hall on the hill still dominates it, and most houses are wood and thatch, but stone houses are appearing and the streets have been straightened. I've even noticed some of the merchants in the town wearing togas. Some Romans visit to trade or buy, and off-duty soldiers from the nearby forts drink in our taverns. Some have set themselves up as business middlemen and live in the villas they favour, and this makes work for our people too.

The Romans demand tribute which Caradog feels is fair, and the family is still rich. He has three sons; fine young men to follow him. The older ones are serious but treat me with respect. They take my ships across many seas and my ships take care of them. Young Ceris is a bit of a dreamer. He is a tall, fine-looking young man who loves ships and sailing. He reads the wind, the sea and the tides as if born to it. I love his smile. He can charm anyone with a flash of his blue eyes and his laugh. He has something about him that people notice and warm to. Despite this, he can be firm and argue any point that he wishes to make. When he hangs around the boatyard he tells me of his dreams to travel far afield like his older brothers do. I remember the trouble he got into when he stowed away on a passage to Ireland, much to his father's annoyance and consternation. That didn't stop him from doing it again! I like the way he doesn't mind helping me, and if he wasn't of our ruler's family he would make a good shipwright. He knows my family and his are intertwined and in a way support each other. I know my place and he know his duties and responsibilities so we understand each other. If my son had lived they would have got on well.

Chapter 4

Ceris

My father and my brothers can talk business for hours. I know I should listen as I know it is important in our lives. My uncle Arthfael is a miserable sod and that makes things worse. I am young and my mind drifts. The shipyard and harbour are my sanctuary. When I can sneak away I go there to see the trees cut into timber, and timbers turned into our ships. I hear the chatter of the men and the noises of the tools; the cutting and the shaping, the violent and the gentle. The smell of new wood and the acidity of the pitch override the salt in the air. I watch old Llyr guiding and teaching the men as they learn their craft. He is old and I can see that he can do less and less himself. His interest remains keen and he can oversee the birth of a ship from the laying of the keel to the planking of the hull and deck. The women of the town create the fabric of the sails and plait the ropes, always according to his instructions. He tells tales from his past, which runs with my story too. His family has stood as witness to our past. I think he knows more than my own family. He says that we cannot have a future without knowing our past.

I am walking along the jetty with Anwen. I had been waiting for her for a while. I was concerned that she might have had difficulty in getting away, and had been sitting dangling my feet off the wooden planking as the sea slipped in and out underneath and the stones sang in the water as the waves receded. I was lost in a daydream when she appeared, and despite my rank, I realised that I was worried that she might not come.

She is a girl of eighteen years of age from the town. Her parents trade in the market area and manage a decent living but I am the son of the ruler and I think they are wary that I will use her. I look at her in profile. I have not been in love before, so the feeling should be strange. Just thinking that makes me realise that perhaps I have fallen in love with her. I know her looks please me; indeed there is little to find fault in. Her face is perfect in its shape and symmetry, her eyes are blue and shine like precious stones, her long hair curls in waves beyond her shoulders, and is a light brown colour with little streaks from the sun. Her shape is lithe and slim, with long legs with sweetly dimpled knees. I realise she is beautiful. She is fun, quick-witted, headstrong and brave.

I see Llyr looking at us. I can read his mind. We are growing up fast and I realise he has been a sort of father to me over the years and now he is seeing the start of me as a man. I am sorry that he lost his son and see that in a way he has seen me as a substitute. He walks away from the growing hull of his latest creation and beckons to me.

'Ceris, what do you see there?'

Taking my eyes off Anwen, I follow his gaze towards a small boat pulled up on the shore. Something about it looks unusual and different and I see that the mast is tall and the sail, which is bundled up along the mast, appears to be looped to two booms. 'I have been talking to the captain of the ship that has come from the great middle sea. Our sails are square and low and take our ships when the wind follows. This means we depend on the oarsmen in other conditions. He was describing larger ships with these sails that can go across and even into the wind.'

'I hear that seas are calmer there and there are only weak tides and currents, although they can have storms as we do that can damage or sink ships.'

I nod, ' I too have heard of such ships but never seen one. They could be mythical like dragons,' I say.

Llyr bursts out laughing, seeing that I am teasing him. 'Here, I have made a small version of this sail on that dinghy. You're not doing anything useful, why don't you try it out?'

I look at Anwen. 'Shall we?'

'Of course,' she agrees. I just knew she would not want to miss out.

We pushed the boat off the beach and into the breaking waves. There is a steady breeze and the sun is shining so it feels like a perfect day to be on the water. We clamber aboard and I used a pair of oars to get us further out. Once we are free and not at risk of being forced back onto the shore, I let the boat float free as I grappled with the sail. Loosening the ties, I pull it up until the top boom rose to the top of the mast and the lower boom lifted free from the deck. Holding the rope attached to the end of it, I moved to the back of the dinghy and grasped the tiller. With Anwen crouched amidships, I gently pulled in the sail and we set off on a course across the wind. The little boat tensed as the sail filled. I could feel her come alive as she quickened. She leaned with the wind and Anwen instinctively moved to the higher side. The sea gurgled under the hull and she seemed to go even faster. I cautiously pushed the tiller away from me and we actually sailed towards the wind. I experimented. Too close and she came upright and lost power as the sail started to flap, turning back the sail tightened again and our speed returned. I repeated that until I had developed a feel for what she was capable of. I realised that we had to turn, and that to tack the boat we would have to get the sail to cross to the other side of it. Warning Anwen, I commenced the manoeuvre and to my surprise and relief it went well. We practised this with Anwen learning to duck under the boom at the right time. She laughed to see how her weight gave stability to our little vessel. She did not appear to be bothered by the spray that came over the bows and I thought that she looked like a beautiful sea goddess. Her thin shift dress was soaked and clung to her body. I could not help but notice how her right breast was outlined by the fabric. Her nipple was pushing against the material, stiffened by wind and sea, creating a picture that was both wild and natural. Truly a sea goddess, I thought. By now we are almost out of sight of the harbour and approaching a small island, and in its shelter I lowered the sail and we lay relaxed and resting after our exertions. She lay curled in my arms in the bottom of the boat. A look of worry passed over her face.

'Do you think we have a future?' she asked.

I found this an awkward question so replied 'Why do

you ask?'

'You are a king's son and I am not of your class. My parents are just shop-keepers.'

I did not know what to say, I did not know what my parents would say, yet I had this vision in my arms. 'Who can tell the future, perhaps we should just learn to enjoy the days we have.'

Was I a coward, I asked myself, was I a coward? We pulled up the sail and returned to the mainland. I could tell that the mood had changed. A small cloud had come across our sun. Arriving at the beach, I had to sort out the sail, dropping and securing it, and getting the oars into position to control our arrival. As Llyr came to greet us and hear of our experience, I was so distracted that I forgot about the rudder and as we grounded there was a loud crack as it smashed against the sea bed.

Anwen left, to dry off, she said. I waved my farewell but she was already walking up away from the harbour. Llyr looked at me quizzically and then his eyes followed the departing figure of Anwen.

'She's a fine girl, isn't she? A lot of spirit in that one. Treat her well,' he said, then looked embarrassed as his impertinence in speaking his mind.

'I know' I said thoughtfully, not minding his comments, 'I know.'

Turning back to the boat having made his point, the old man asked 'What did you think?'

I realised he would have liked the experience himself and replied. 'It really works. With the sail pulled in, she will go into the wind, and away from the wind there is a large sail exposed to push her. It's as you said, can you imagine this on a larger ship?'

Llyr smiled and said 'Perhaps one day.'

I heard a hail in the distance and realised that Grifud had come to reclaim me for the family. Smiling apologetically, I took my leave.

Chapter 5

Caradog

After the night of celebrations, the atmosphere between the two families is one of harmony. The year is getting older, and it is the time for planting crops and breeding the animals. It is also a time for trade: the winter storms have passed and the better weather makes voyaging safer. The two families take a stroll through the town. Aine grimaces at a pool of vomit at the side of one road, but Caradog laughs. Few townspeople are visible on the streets.

'Sign of a good celebration' says Brychan, 'let's hope it brings luck for the next year.'

They start to return to the hall, climbing up the stone road that leads up the hill. As the families prepare to take leave of each other, there happens an event that will change their lives forever.

On the hill opposite the great hall appears a troop of men on horseback. As they get closer they can see the Roman uniforms and armour, and when closer still they can identify the leader, riding ahead of the main body. They descend the hill, then ride up through the town until they reach the hall. Their leader stares at the dragon banner, dismounts, throws the reins to one of his men and stalks up to where Caradog.and Arthfael are standing. They can see that he is a physically imposing man with the hard weather-worn face of a warrior, not an administrator.

'I am Quintus Aurelius Silvanus, envoy of your governor and also represent general Maximian, overall commander of the armies of Gaul and Britain. Having inspected the south, the east and the north I am now here. Who is in charge?'

Caradog steps forward saying 'I am Caradog ap Einudd and I rule here, and this is my brother Arthfael who rules in Siluria. You are welcome but have missed our spring celebration.'

Quintus appears to be wrong-footed with such a reception. Caradog knows he rules by the grace of Rome but expects his family line to be respected.

'I have spoken with Paulinus and he has shown me the ledgers and told me of you. I am surprised to see your town looking rich. Compared to many you seem to have learned from our influence and I even see some soldiers here who from their appearance' he looks disapprovingly 'are not on duty.'

Caradog replies 'We are traders, we provide goods for those who wish to buy and our town has prospered. We pay our taxes and seek to get along with Rome.'

'I have seen the records and can find no fault although Paulinus was lax to the point of generosity, I fear.'

Perceiving a threat, Arthfael interrupts to introduce himself and to play for time and ingratiate themselves the two brothers introduce their family members. Quintus listens patiently but gets down to business.

'I am not minded to increase your taxes at present. I have seen throughout the country that some of your kingdoms are struggling to provide even the meagre demands that Rome makes. Not yours, of course. You are far away from London, which makes inspections difficult. I realise I have to take a lot on trust, and I am not a trusting man.'

He glares while Caradog and Arthfael look uncomfortable, to their shame. They expected to be treated with some respect, not humiliated in front of their families.

'However, there is something I want of you to ensure your cooperation. Since the time of Julius Agricola, your first governor two hundred years ago, it has sometimes been required of rulers allowed responsibility that they provide a son to serve Rome. Rome needs warriors and I know you have sent some of your people to be soldiers when we have required it, but we can give training those who can lead. A son from each of your will ensure your good intentions and loyalty to Rome.'

'You are taking them as hostages. I have only one son' shouts Arthfael.

'You might say that, I wouldn't quite as I know I can now count on your cooperation, can't I, so there's no need for threats' replies Quintus, obviously not intimidated by Arthfael's anger. 'You should make another son' he adds casually and carelessly.

He draws himself up, flexing his authority by accentuating his military bearing. 'I expect you will get them back safe and sound'.

He looks around. Staring at Xander he says 'You will not make much of a warrior but I will take you to London where you will get an education and learn about our empire'.

He turns and surveys the sons of Caradog, and passing over the two fully grown older ones his eyes settle on Ceris. 'You, I believe, might make a soldier, I will take you to join my general Maximian's forces in Gaul. You will get to see some action, I promise.'

Turning to Caradog, he says 'My men and I will be staying at the fort a few miles down the road. I have some business there. We will return in four or five days. Have these young men ready to leave, I will bring horses for them.'

Chapter 6

Ceris

I crossed the great channel in a Roman military ship. It was much bigger than our ships of trade and powered by dozens of oars. There was a great ram at the bow and I wondered how fast the rowers could go. I had heard tales of sea warfare in the great middle sea from visiting traders, and tried to imagine the scenes as these huge ships clashed. The crossing had been quick and calm and we disembarked in a group and were marched in a north-easterly direction shown to me by the stars to the military encampment in Gaul for training. We were joined by other recruits to the army, some willing, some in it for the money and prospects and others like me who had no say in the matter. We were a ragged bunch when we arrived and were lined up for the disapproval of the centurion in charge of training, a fierce and angry man called Claudius Albinus who looked at us with a glare that suggested we were an imposition on his time. He sneered at us and looked askance.

'Where in the depths of Neptune's arsehole did they drag you up from? I've never seen such a shower.'

Looking around I felt some sympathy for his view as he surveyed a mass of humanity; dusty, dirty and footsore recruits, some hunched and huddled and from many parts of the empire and beyond.

'Stand up straight! You are privileged to join the great fighting machine of the Roman army. What it will make of you I cannot say. Some of you look even more useless than a wooden sword.'

We stood in a line and I tried to show a bearing according to my background. He frowned as he stalked up and down the collection of recruits. 'You, what is your name and where are you from?'

'My name is Ceris ap Caradog and I am from a kingdom in Wales in the island of Britain.'

'That means nothing now. I hear the place is a shithole anyway. Welcome to the Roman army. You at least look like a military specimen. I might be able to do something with you.'

I continued to stand straight despite my anger at his insult to my country. Ignoring his glare I hoped he picked on someone else. He put his face up against mine. I feel the heat of his anger and smell his foetid breath. 'Are you scared of me?'

I replied 'I am not sure yet.'

He said 'You should be and will be. I will march you into the ground, fight you into the ground and try to make a soldier out of you.'

I met his gaze and said 'Maybe I will fear you, I will

let you know.'

At this impudence the recruit next to me stifled a giggle. I had noticed that he had a demeanour that suggested a degree of learning and breeding.

The old centurion turned on him. 'Another stroppy one are you? And who are you anyway?

'I am Decimus, here to do my duty to Rome.'

'I will make sure you do that, sonny. I've met your type before, here to gain respect for your family through blood and mud.'

After he had finished insulting everyone down the line, we had to run for several miles before we could relax and find something to eat from the canteen tent. Exhausted, we collected and ate something unrecognisable and I sat down next to Decimus.

'I think we may have drawn more attention to ourselves than was wise.'

We talked about our backgrounds. Decimus was from a minor family of Rome but exuded importance and confidence. I did not mention that I was from a ruling family as part of me was seeing no comparison in this new world.

As we trained we became very fit. My body stopped aching and my muscles grew bulky. We could march, run and handle the shield and gladius. It's fair and not boastful to say that Decimus and I were among the best of our group. Some of them asked for help or advice and some resented us. Albinus grudgingly accepted our growing professionalism and tended to lay off us with the criticism and punishments. Decimus and I made friends with some of the officers, and we discussed strategy, tactics and tricks. I heard about many great battles of the past, such as when a Carthaginian called Hannibal ran riot though the lands of Italy and slaughtered many Roman soldiers. I learned too that while he won his victories through skill, there were many faults in the Roman leadership that hindered their defence. Only once these were dealt with did Rome eventually triumph. At the end of our training, Albinus told us we had done him proud.

He looked at me and said 'I think I have made a Roman soldier out of you. You can't carry a barbarian name.'

I protested that I was from a ruling family but he said that did not mean anything. From now on I should take the closest Romanised name of Carausius, and from that point everyone, from the ordinary soldiers to the officers, insisted on calling me by that name. As it was often used with respect, Carausius is who I became. I think Albinus felt he was instrumental in our development as soldiers, for which he probably was. Decimus and I took leading roles in our minor skirmishing with the barbarian tribes and after two years we were promoted to centurions and given a hundred soldiers of our own to command and train. As the legion pushed north, I felt that it was too far for the barbarians for whom loss of territory and pride would force them to make a stand. I thought of my own people and how their resistance to the Romans ended in the foothills of Snowdonia when they could retreat no more.

Maximian surveyed his troops. We were ranked in blocks and stood to attention with our uniforms clean and our armour polished. Our armourers were skilled at making weapons and sharpening them so they could pierce even metal. All was prepared for battle. The evening before he had addressed the assembled soldiers with stuff about the glory of the Roman empire, bringing civilisation to barbarians, capturing slaves, and the footsteps of Julius Caesar. Decimus and I looked at each other. What he meant was that a battle was coming so he could enhance his reputation. He was a big angry man and he would use our lives to do it. At the dinner afterwards he discussed tactics with his commander and looked searchingly at the junior officers. Finally he had left and we could get some sleep.

A misty dawn greeted us as the legion assembled. I was to take my century onto a forested ridge on the right of a shallow valley to be held as reserves. The main advance was to follow the course of the valley. Some of my men grumbled that they could miss the fighting but I silenced them.

'We will wait here in this brushwood and conceal ourselves. Helmets off, stay hidden. When the sun comes up fully I don't want our position given away by reflections'.

Scouts had reported that a large mass of barbarian soldiers was gathering beyond the valley. This was far more than just a skirmishing party and told us that a battle was ahead.

Decimus's troops were in the forefront of the main group which slowly formed up and occupied the width of the valley. A river meandered to the left and I noted that the ground there was marshy. As the legion assembled I marvelled at the discipline of the soldiers. We were all armed with a light throwing spear, a gladius and a dagger. With their red-painted shields held in front of them, the men in the valley gave the appearance of an armoured wall as they stood silently in ranks. The Eagle, the legion's standard, was held proudly in the centre. It symbolised the honour of the legion and the might of Rome. How insignificant was my country when compared with this demonstration of invincible power.

Maximian, observing the placement of the legion, signalled his commander to advance. As the lines took a step forwards, we heard noises from the barbarians. Warned of the advanced by their scouts, they started to move forwards. As they came into view, I saw a wild bunch of savage looking men armed with spears, swords and carrying small round shields. Their bodies were painted in blue dyes and their hair was long as were the beards of many, both embellished with objects like beads. As they bellowed war cries some started to run at the advancing Roman line. The legionaries had been beating their swords against their shields to sound a defiant marching rhythm, but withdrew to lock shields to resist the wave of attackers. I noted a lack of coordination or leadership in their charge and saw the first crazed attackers cut down by spears thrown by the first rank of Romans. Undeterred, the barbarians continued to hurl themselves at the shield walls. Some of their spears flew overhead and found their targets, burying themselves in Roman chests. As a Roman fell, the lines closed up and their advance continued inexorably. Suddenly I saw a change in the barbarian attack. A sort of organisation seemed to happen, against all the wild behaviour that was usual. A barbarian, clearly a leader, dressed in a short fur coat and carrying a sword, was rallying his men and the attack changed. They made a short line and seemed to act in pairs. Some were armed with long-handled axes and fought in tandem with ones armed with short spears, shorter than the throwing ones that they had used to some effect. As they closed on the Romans, the axes were brought down like hooks over the shields of the Romans, which were then pulled forcibly downwards. As the torsos of the soldiers were exposed the short spears were used to stab them. If the manoeuvre with the axe failed, the spears were used against their legs. So effective was this, the centre of the Roman line started to break. Off balance and with the barbarians keeping out of the stabbing range of the short gladius swords, the advance faltered, then gaps started to appear. I looked on in horror. This mighty, polished, disciplined Roman war machine could fail. The line started to retreat, leaving Roman bodies for the barbarians to climb over. I could see Decimus trying to rally his soldiers to cover the withdrawal and protect the Eagle standard. Its bearer was vulnerable and the barbarian leader was pushing his way towards it as the mass pushed through.

The retreat of the Roman line had left my men behind the line of the fighting, and seeing my opportunity I commanded my men to don their helmets and descend into the valley. They ran, with me in the lead, and fell on the barbarians from behind, taking them by surprise. Hacking with our short swords, we cut their way through, blood flying, slipping on limbs and guts, until we halted the barbarian advance. Iron clashed with steel, and both slashed against wooden shields on their way to their final aim of flesh. I felt the blood lust and battle rage that drove men to kill. Kill or be killed, I thought, we must gain a victory. My sword smashed down and spilt the head of one barbarian. Grey jelly poured from his skull down his face as he remained standing for several seconds before he fell. The noise of the battle was deafening; shouts, howls and cries of pain, thumps, grunts and squelches. Decimus saw that the barbarian attack had faltered and called on his men to fight. He turned on the huge barbarian warrior who was wrestling with the Eagle standard and with a massive swing of his sword almost decapitated him. Blood sprayed around as his body fell. Decimus stepped over it and rallied his men. Sandwiched between two lines of enraged Romans, many barbarians were slaughtered. I had too few men to stop a retreat of those who could, and no strength left to chase them, so we could only watch as the cloaked leader and a few of his men retreated at a desperate run. The sounds of the battlefield had changed in only minutes from cries of defiance to shrieks of pain from the injured and dying.

Maximian was conducting a review of the battle.

'That looked a bit of a close run thing for a while, didn't it?' He turned to his commander. 'I assume you decided to draw the barbarians into the centre to trap them?'

The commander hesitated briefly, and this was noted by Maximian. 'And how many men did we lose?'

Before he could reply, he turned to me. 'Centurion, when did you get the signal to leave the hill and attack? Didn't you leave it a bit late?' He turned then looked back at me 'Don't worry, I know exactly what happened. I'm not stupid and you not only showed initiative but saved the Eagle and the honour of the legion.'

When I left I was greeted by soldiers who realised I had saved the day and possibly their own lives. A pair of them started beating their shields and shouting 'Hail Carausius'. They were joined by more, similarly shouting 'Hail Carausius' until glared at and silenced by their officers.

Later in his tent, Maximian was shouting at his commander. 'You nearly lost the day. If it hadn't been for that young man from Britain things would have been different and you would have been disgraced.'

'I can only apologise, your Excellency, I will not fail you again.'

'You certainly won't, I could require you to fall on your sword now. If you fail me again I will have you publicly executed. Now fetch me those two young centurions, you owe your life to them.'

Maximian was lounging on a sofa, regarding carefully these two young men. He was concerned about the sudden popularity of Carausius and the regard with which people seem to hold him. He recognised his physical strength, his good looks and military skill and realised that he was experiencing jealousy. This thought stopped his train of thinking and an idea formed.

Firstly he spoke to Decimus. 'We have trained you well, and do not hold you responsible for our line breaking. The way you rallied your troops afterwards is what impressed me. It seems to me that these barbarians deserve some credit for their tactics. I hope this is not how they will fight in the future, but we must prepare. We cannot easily get our war machines into these terrains so fighting will always be at close quarters. I am promoting you to second in command of this legion and you will be in charge of training the men to be aware of this way of attack and how to counter it in future. Dismiss!'

He turned to me. After staring straight into my eyes, he said. 'I acknowledge the credit that is owed to you. You have the thanks of the legion and Rome. How long have you served us?'

I replied 'I have been here for three full years now.'

Maximian put on a thoughtful expression. 'You are a long way from your homelands. I think maybe it is time to give you leave from your duties here so that you can return to your family. You have earned this'.

I could have seen no end to his time with this army so smiled in thanks.

'But remember that I might call on you again. Take

your wages, proceed to Boulogne and take ship to your own land.'

I did not notice the threat implied in the last sentence and was exhilarated at the thought of going home. I took my leave of Decimus and his soldiers.

'I will miss you all and wish you well for the future. Decimus, we have had some adventures in these years and you have been a good friend. Take care, and (lowering my voice) I wouldn't put any trust in anything that Maximian says.'

I rode off, hearing a few cries of 'Hail Carausius' to see me on my way.

Chapter 7

Xander

To be honest, I was not sure what to think when I was taken from my home and sent to London. I had no doubts of my status as a hostage, for that what it was. I knew I was being taken to ensure my father's cooperation. I knew as well that he did not make a good impression on Quintus. At first I was terrified at leaving everything I knew. I had not left the lands of my father and his brother before and I was travelling among a group of men who ignored me and looked down on me as if I was nothing, although I was a ruler's son. Even Quintus, the man responsible for my plight was distant and barely spoke. As we journeyed, we slept at small Roman forts where I was left among the animals in the stables. The towns got bigger and I started to see more people, larger buildings and evidence of wealth. The people were well-dressed and clean, with buckles, clips and jewellery that appeared to be as artistic as much as they were functional. Roman soldiers were everywhere, on duty or off, and it became clear who was in charge. Life went on for the people, though, as if they accepted their subordinate condition.

As we finally entered London, my mood became one of curiosity followed by amazement. On the outskirts there were the usual collections of wooden round houses, but as we approached the walls of the city I almost could not believe my eyes. We passed through a large arched gate manned by sentries with soldiers on the ramparts. The streets got wider and the buildings! Made from smooth stones and fired clay roofing, they were from a different world. Where we had buildings made from stone, they were from rocks from the sea or dug up from the soil and stuck together with mortar from lime. The Roman buildings shone in the sunlight and the joins between these stones were barely visible. These streets went on and on, paved with cobbles on which the horses hooves clattered and echoed. There were open spaces, parks and meeting places. Even the merchants' premises and hostelries were bigger and cleaner than anything I had seen before.

After what felt like several miles we arrived at the house where I was to stay. It was a grand stone house with three levels, and as Quintus led me through the doorway I saw the walls painted with what I learned were classical Roman themes. I walked on floors made from small tiles set in cement that again portrayed pictures of gods, animals and battles. I was dumbstruck and barely recall being introduced to the family. I had been told that Flavius Valentinus was a senior administrator of finance in the Roman government and his wife Livia kept house and entertained for him. Quintus left swiftly, having delivered me as planned. From his military point of view, he had completed his task and fulfilled his duty. I wondered if I would ever see him again.

Livia said 'Welcome, we have been expecting you and you must be tired after your journey.'

She was a tall good-looking woman with, I thought, a kind face. Quintus had mentioned that she had a son of about my age and I could feel that she would be a good mother to him. I wondered how she would regard me. I looked at my dusty and faded clothes and she studied me closely. 'You will see that things are different here but you will soon settle in.'

She clearly did not regard my hostage position as important and to my surprise I felt greeted like a guest.

'You will meet our son Magnus later when he has finished his lessons, but first you must take a bath and I will find something for you to wear.'

She led me through the house into another room where a tiled bath already full of water was set into the floor. Steam arose from the surface. I was astonished, and she must have thought my reaction was fear.

'Don't worry' she laughed, 'We Romans are very hygienic. Bathing regularly is part of our lifestyle. There are large communal baths in the city, where men and women bath in groups and meet just for conversations.'

I thought of how we cleansed ourselves back in my home. Streams and waterfalls were our facilities, always so cold that washing was quick. No time to stop and talk there! The richer folk might have wooden tubs but it took servants a long time to carry enough water to fill them.

'Take off those clothes and I will have some clean ones sent to you.'

She sensed my hesitation and said that she would leave me alone. She turned and left the room so I pulled off my filthy clothes and slid into the warm water. I had never felt anything like it. I thought that I could stay forever in here, then saw how the water discoloured from the dirt that came off my skin. There was a bar of oily soap and I used it, and I became clean while the water darkened. I was embarrassed by this and could see no way to let the water out. The door opened and a vision walked in. I was sixteen years old and I knew about girls, of course. I had heard talk about their schemes and wiles and had seen how some looked at my cousin Ceris and tried to catch his eye. I knew I was not particularly handsome nor strong like him and my old feelings of envy briefly returned. I thought that even when his age I would not be looked at like that. The vision carried in her arms a white robe and underclothes, obviously for me. She wore a long tunic and her hair was braided and shining and her pretty face broke into a smile when she saw my plight. She handed me a towel and waited. My face became redder and hot and she laughed and turned away. I quickly got out, dried myself and slipped on the underclothes.

She said 'Are you ready?'

She turned back and saw me struggling with the toga. Still laughing she adjusted it, smiled and left with my old clothes. I wondered if she was a daughter of the house but learned that she was a slave girl called Chresima who had been with the family for several years. I learned that there were two other slaves who helped with domestic chores. They had simple accommodation at the back of the house and I was surprised to learn that they had the freedom to leave the house, both for errands and shopping but to meet others in their situation. The slaves that my family had had in their distant past were usually captured in wars, worked hard and treated worse than the family animals. I had supposed that was their fault for losing.

I studied my new self. I was miles from my home and in a world that was unrecognisable. I felt as if I had moved to another planet. Later the master of the house returned from work.

He greeted me with a curious look. 'I wondered what we were taking on, but you look quite at home.'

Valentinus was a man of presence, handsome and clearly educated and wealthy. His bearing was one of authority and I could see how he held an important position in the government.

I said 'Thank you Sir, I have been made welcome but this home is not what I am used to.'

'Quintus is a hard man and you may feel that you are being held hostage against your father's behaviour. I assure you that I see our role as introducing you to our Roman world so see it as an opportunity. You will attend daily lessons with my son Magnus, who is of similar age to you, and when and if you show talent you will come and work with me.'

I was reassured to hear this, and he said 'Quintus says you are a quick learner; whether that is a fact or an order we will find out.' Clearly I was being treated as part of the family and joined them for meals and learned how to eat at table.

As the weeks went by, my speech improved and my ignorance started to lift. Magnus was a pleasant boy and we got on well. He had the confident air of his social class which concealed a wicked sense of mischief. He played tricks on people for which I sometimes got the blame, but we became like a pair of conspirators, humorously taking on the world. I had told him of my father's lands and that I was a ruler's son but he was not impressed. Immersed in the might of Rome as he was, I think I would have thought the same. In lessons I was taught to read and write, and we covered mathematics, poetry, philosophy and of course the history of the empire. I was told that my name Xander was from Alexander, a Macedonian who had built a large empire in the days before even the Romans. In Roman my name was Allectus, by which I was forever known. Our tutor liked to set tests to assess our progress and I was pleased to gain high marks. They were sometimes higher than those of Magnus but he did not seem to mind. We competed at sports with other boys and learned some exercises in fighting. I felt fit and healthy, we were now seventeen years old and felt immortal. One day, Magnus saw me looking at Chresima the slave girl. He winked and I looked away. I thought she looked like a goddess as portrayed on the walls and in the floors. I started to blush and he laughed and said 'Later'.

'What do you mean?' I asked but he stared at me trying to hide an embarrassing bulge in my clothing then laughed again.

'Later' he said again.

That night I learned what later meant. Chresima came to my room, slipped into my bed and I learned my first lesson in love.

After two years it was considered that I had excelled in my education and that it was time to go into the wider world. I thought less and less about my home as I gained more in London. I realised that part of this education was removing me from my roots, while offering me much more than I had ever had at home.

Valentinus took me to his offices. Here was the administrative heart of the Roman province of Britain. I saw how records were kept; accounts of costs, charges, income and expenditure of the regions. Taxes were taken, tributes and charges for punishment logged. I saw how goods were traded; grains, animals, minerals had negotiated values. I saw how the greater empire bought grains from Britain and minerals. For the first time I saw how trading families like my uncle Caradog's carried goods to and fro, all part of the great business of empire. I also noted that the lands of my father merited but a line or two in the great ledgers of Rome.

When four years had passed, I was told that my time in London was ending and that I had permission to travel home. I realised that, having yearned for home in the beginning, I did not want to leave. It was part of the hostage taking that I would be returned so that had to happen. Sadly, I took my farewells, mounted a horse to join an group travelling west, and left London, where I had lived, learned and loved.

The journey felt slow and my heart did not quicken as I approached my parents' great hall. Nothing seemed to have changed and it was like going back centuries of time. As I dismounted, my father came out, looked at his only son dressed in a short toga like a young Roman, and greeted me with a sneer.

Chapter 8

Darius

I was taken from my parents after a Roman invasion of the lands they called Mesopotamia. My family had wealth and status but that counted for nothing after defeat in war. I think I was about seven years of age and I never saw them again. They may have been killed or sent away as punishment for being on the losing side. I had had some basic schooling that stood me apart from other children and orphans so I was placed with the family of the newly appointed Roman governor. As a young slave boy, I was given tasks from dawn to dusk. Cleaning, sweeping, polishing; as they became established they gained so many more possessions that became soiled in the sand and dust. The building grew too, extended into more rooms, a large salon and several courtyards. This of course meant more to clean. I can't say I was treated badly. I was fed, clothed and had a comfortable but small room to sleep. I grew taller of course and being stronger followed as I was constantly working. I was given different tasks when another small boy was taken on. He looked so young and lost I tried to teach him what to do when I had time. There were stables, carriages and even a war chariot to look after now. As part of exercising the horses I learned to ride, something that gave me pleasure. From being controlled in all my activities I enjoyed guiding these large strong animals to do my bidding. I realised that the family thought that I looked presentable in some way. Unlike them, my skin was very dark, not through the sun that burned theirs red, but as it naturally was. It was smooth with no scars or marks, and I saw that this gave me something that excited the curiosity of visitors. Not because I was unusual; most of the people around in the fields and towns were similar, but because I was seen as more civilised, more Romanised in some way. I dressed in ways familiar to them and spoke their language. Approaching about eighteen years of age by now, as I estimated, I also was regarded as handsome and had grown taller than many men. I saw my features in reflections and could agree that there was a pleasant symmetry to my features and my body was lithe and muscular. I was often used to serve food to guests and given fine clothes to wear. Some of the ladies looked at me in a quizzical way and I dared not to wonder what they were thinking.

One evening I was finishing clearing tables after a large group of dignitaries and their wives had taken large amounts of wine. They were all about to retire to the salon to continue their discussions (I could see in the faces of most of the wives that they found this boring). I knelt to pick up a glass from the floor next to a padded bench where a lady was reclining. She had been drinking, her face was flushed and her tunic was falling off her shoulders I felt a hand slide up under my tunic. I jumped up in surprise, dropping the glass. I saw her husband returning from the doorway in concern as she cried out. She claimed that I had touched her chest as I knelt, something that no servant or slave would be allowed to do. I looked her in the eyes and said that I would not and I had not. It was to no avail. The husband was important and indignant, my owner was humiliated and I was dragged away and thrown into a stinking stable that was locked after me.

I was left there until the following evening when I was

brought before my master. I tried to explain but he was angry and unprepared to believe me. I could not understand, I looked through my tears at the man I had served for most of my life, but he said I had to be punished severely for my presumption and would be sent to the galleys.

I was left dirty and unwashed in my stable until I was handed over like a dog to a passing Roman military unit. My arms were tied and with a few dozen other miserable souls we were marched through the desert for days. Our feet blistered as our shoes fell apart. No consideration was shown by the soldiers, it seemed they did not care in what state we arrived, or even if we arrived at all. Two or three collapsed on the way and when clearly unable to carry on, their throats were cut and they were left for the vultures and great grey wolves to feast on. Hit with sticks if we slowed, it appeared that we made good progress that satisfied them and at last after an eternity we reached the great port of Seleucia. I had never seen anything like this. We looked down upon a vista of blue sea with a great town and harbour. Having never seen the sea, although I had been heard tell of it, of course, it appeared tamed by massive jetties against which enormous galleys were tied. There were streets, stone buildings and a bazaar to be seen on our passage to the harbour itself, but we were dragged and pushed into a dark hot building, thrown some food and drink and left to catch our breath and await our fate.

The following day, the door was opened and we were forced blinking into the daylight. Soldiers surrounded us and a brutal man with a whip walked up and down. He seemed prepared to use it on us so we stood as straight as our painful and blistered bodies would allow. Being one of the youngest and still fittest, I was selected for a large warship whose side was pieced by so many oar holes I could not count them. I heard from one of the tongues that I could understand that the ship was leaving for Rome itself, with a group of soldiers and some civic dignitaries who were returning gratefully to civilization. I saw that the galley slaves, for that is what we were, were chained to their benches in case we rebelled. We outnumbered the crew so I suppose that was a real fear. Some of the oarsmen were well-muscled, and as I discovered had been stuck on ships for years. My heart fell as I realised that this was my fate too. All my dreams of making my own life and fortune seemed to wither in my heart.

With much shouting, the great ship was pushed away from the jetty. I followed the example of the others and pushed my great oar through its hole and wrestled it onto its pivot. To the beat of a drum we arranged our strokes in unison. To the experienced it was easy but to me, just dealing with the heaviness of the oar was enough. A gangmaster patrolled the walkway between the two sides, looking for those who were not coordinated or flagging. I was both and received several whiplashes across my back to add to my troubles. As the days passed the ship called at several ports, and crew, passengers and cargo changed. I learned that wars often broke out between Rome and its rivals, and one day at sea, I found out how it was to fight on a war galley. Shouts broke out and it was quickly passed around that possibly hostile ships had been seen. We were sailing in the company of several other Roman warships; I could glance them occasionally through my oar hatch. Suddenly there was a call for more speed as our great galley turned. The drum beats became faster in response to drive us on. I could not know what was going on, of course, but I realised we were in trouble as the soldiers were called to formation as an enemy ship was getting near. I sensed panic as the ship lurched into a sharp turn. How near I only realised when there was a great crash, followed by the splintering of wood, and a huge dripping bronze ram piercing the side of our ship just ahead of my position. Several oarsmen were crushed, at least two dead and a couple were screaming in pain as blood poured from them. Some water had poured in but luckily most of the damage was above the waterline. We could only sit and listen helplessly as the soldiers fought on the deck above and blood that appeared from everywhere turned the sea around our feet to the colour of wine.

After a while it became clear that we had won. The great ram withdrew as the enemy ship floated away. Silence fell as the crew set about rescuing our ship. Our crew unchained us out of necessity and knowing we shared the risk, and moved everything possible to the other side of the ship. As it tilted away, a sailcloth patch was nailed across the splintered hole and we proceeded slowly on our course to Rome with half the rowers and the rest bailing out the water. On arrival, the slaves were again separated and locked in a room, this time with a courtyard. I didn't get to see anything of Rome, to my regret. Ten of us were told we were taking a boat to the channel between Gaul and Britain. We joined ten others and set off in a smaller ship that was more open to the elements but meant we could actually see out, which was mostly grey, choppy sea below a heavy grey sky.

I could see no end to my life like this. We rowed the ship again and again across the channel, carrying soldiers and civilians. Sometimes there was a favourable wind and we could rest while the sail was hoisted. I was curious to learn how the water moved backwards and forwards each day. I was told it was something to do with the moon, but as I had seen the moon in the great central sea, it did not seem to have this effect there. I got to know my fellow slaves. What a mixture; some taken in war, some criminals, some facing banishment or execution and choosing this life. Having been brought up with Romans, I could speak and understand their language quite well. Others I could not, although with gestures and signs we could just about get on. There was a large muscular man who the others seemed to call Grunt, as that is what he did, but it turned out his tongue had been torn from his mouth as a punishment. We had the scars, we had the calluses and all in all, as we were together in our lives, we managed to get on well and help each other when we could.

Chapter 9

Carausius

I arrived at the Roman port of Boulogne and spent some of my wages on staying in an inn while awaiting a suitable ship to cross the great channel to the naval base at Dover. Seeing my uniform, the locals identified me as Roman and some were wary to talk with me. From others I discovered that there was no real news. There was certainly no chance of hearing anything of my far-flung homeland, so I explored the town and the fortified harbour built on the estuary of a great river. I marvelled at its sheer size and could not imagine it ever being successfully attacked.

Finally, the day arrived where there was a small military ship sailing for Britain. When I say small, it was similar in size to our trading ships but dwarfed by three great triremes; fearsome battleships powered by banks of oars and built with massive bronze rams and boarding platforms. I imagined the sight of several of these in action and wondered what could be ranged against them. As I waited to board, I was joined by Quintus and his escort who were returning to London.

'I hear you have excelled yourself and caught the eye of the emperor himself.'

I replied 'Yes, but now I am returning to my home.'

'You may think you earned this but Maximian is wary of those who become popular,' he replied with a warning look.

I said 'But you are his man, you have served him for years.'

He shrugged, 'Because of this I know how he thinks. You don't get anything for nothing from him and if you cross him you will pay in one form or another. Anyway, enjoy your freedom, I think I chose you well.'

We boarded the ship and stowed our belongings. The vessel had graceful lines with a short mast and square sail. It was powered by twenty oarsmen and as I studied them closely I could see that they were a mixed bunch of men of various sizes and skin colour.

Quintus saw me looking and said 'Don't feel sorry for them. These men are here for various reasons, some captured in wars, some criminals who did not merit execution and others who chose this rather than be killed or mutilated.'

I noted the long chains that ran the length of the ship, shackling the foot of each one by a metal strap around an ankle. Some of the slaves looked subdued, but one stood out. He was dark-skinned and had the same look as some of the soldiers I had served with who came from the eastern part of the empire near the lands of this new god who was becoming popular with some Romans. He seemed to have a quiet dignity that did not fit his circumstances. At home we had received the emissaries of this man who claimed to be the son of god for many years. I had also learned about the Roman gods while in the army; my people worshipped various deities but I didn't believe in such things. I felt the powers of nature such as wind and rain and only they could touch my soul.

When the ship was ready the seamen cast off the lines and we were rowed slowly out of the estuary. The sky was clear and the sun was shining, but there was a stiff breeze from the east and my sailor's nose smelt salt and dampness on the wind. The captain did not seem concerned so I settled down to my place as a passenger. The rowers settled into a gentle rhythm and I was starting to slip into sleep when I was alerted to a change in the ship's motion. Opening my eyes I could see that the sky had darkened, and the ships movement was pitching and yawing and the rowers were starting to struggle. As one set of oars pulled in the water the other side left it completely. Some rowers were slipping on their benches and the coordination of an experienced set of oarsmen was lost. The small sail that was not contributing much was bulging and billowing and contributing to the instability of the ship.

The wind whipped around the ship and heavy rain started lashing down. The rain drops stung our faces and visibility disappeared. The captain was struggling at his steering oar and the motion of the ship got worse, rearing out of the water at one point and crashing down again the next. Waves were battering the ship, drenching us with spray and I saw with dismay that water was filling the bilges. The mighty strong man that we saw as Quintus was looking frightened and green, while several of his escort were vomiting copiously. Unable to reach over the sides of the ship, this was ending up in the bilges too. With every movement of the ship, a wave of water would wash over the feet of the slaves. There were panicky looks everywhere and it was clear that we were now lost and in danger of sinking. Suddenly a great wave hit the ship and two rowers were smashed in their chests by the handles of their oars. One was obviously dead and the other started vomiting blood. The ship slewed round and a great cracking noise told of the breaking of the mast. The sail fell across the ship and went partially over the side. At this violent movement, there was a cry of alarm and the captain was swept overboard into the teeming sea. I looked around. Quintus was hanging onto the side as if his life depended on it. His soldiers seemed barely conscious. He caught my eye and for the first time I saw desperation in his and that he was in a situation that he could not control.

I said 'Make me captain.'

He looked at me, not understanding.

I said again 'Make me captain.'

With bemusement on his face, he said 'All right, I appoint you captain.'

Through this I had absolute control and authority and shouted at the soldiers to rouse themselves if they wanted to live. Several started to move and I gave instructions to start bailing out the bilges. They had their helmets and despite the blood and vomit in the water, they started to carry this out. To another I ordered 'Unchain the slaves.'

Quintus looked alarmed.

I said 'We are all in this situation, and they cannot save themselves against the movement of the sea. You have seen what happened to those who couldn't get themselves out of the way.' I added 'I'm sure they are not in a condition to take revenge on Rome, and I now have your authority to run this ship, don't I?'

I took the steering oar at the stern and wrestled to control the wild movements of the ship. One soldier made to cut away the rigging that was holding the sail that was strewn across the across the ship and dragging in the water. I shouted at him to stop.

'This is stabilising the ship and we can do more by trailing more ropes from the other side'.

This we did and slowly the movement of the ship became calmer. The storm continued to blow and I organised six oarsmen to row gently to keep the ship on track to who knows where. As one became exhausted I used a soldier in his place. I looked at Quintus who had recovered enough to give a look which said not to involve him! I knew we were being pushed westwards but there was no sight of land and the great channel grew much wider. While there was little chance of going aground, the great tides were pushing us too.

Eventually the storm blew itself out. We drifted through mists, fog and drizzle until the rain stopped, the seas calmed and the sun even started to shine weakly. I was not sure how many days had elapsed as days and nights had merged into one. We had a damaged ship, two slaves had died and we slid their bodies into the sea. The dark man who appeared to take a role as their leader muttered some words, I assume of religious significance, and several others joined in. As visibility returned I could see a dark sliver of land off the starboard side. We were still being forced westwards by the wind and tide, and although we had some control with the oars, we were too exhausted to do much to resist this. As the conditions continued to ease, with rotation of oarsmen and at a slow speed I was able to edge towards the coast, hoping to spot some landmarks that might tell me where we were. I could not hear noises of waves breaking on a shore so I felt safe, but not very sound.

I saw two headlands with what looked like a sandy beach between them. I knew the charts that my family had drawn over the generations and decided that we were way down to the west of the country. Spirits rose as we got closer and as we started to hear the sound of breaking waves of the shore, and finally beached the ship on solid ground. We clambered off and fell on the sand. We were burnt by the sun, parched and coated in salt, with blisters on our hands from the oars. After what felt like hours of lying in an exhausted pile of humanity, Quintus was the first to rally. He stood up, looked at the huddle of slaves, and called on his escort to get ready to leave. He looked at me.

'I believe I, no we, owe you for saving our lives. I really thought that this was the end and that I would meet my ancestors'.

I nodded, and as our eyes met I knew that he knew that

I had seen him at his most vulnerable. Knowing he would hold that against me at some time, I nodded again. He gathered his escort and they started to march slowly across the beach to the land. His last words were 'You're still the captain. Fix the ship.'

With Quintus gone, I took stock of the situation. The slaves looked at me, and the tall dark one who I learned was called Darius said 'Master?'

I replied 'I am not your master.'

'You saved our lives, you released us from our chains and we are in land we do not know. I know these men, we have spent much time together and we want you to lead us.'

Several others nodded and a babble of languages seemed to agree. I said again 'I am not your master, I have no need of slaves.'

'Then we will follow you willingly. We know you are a great warrior who is not Roman and have no wish to take revenge of you.'

What do I do? I thought. And what do I do with this collection of strangers? As is reading my mind, Darius asked 'Where will we go?'

The answer in my mind was to return to my home so I said 'We will go to the land of my father.' There was no reply so I said 'We must gather our strength, repair the ship as best we can and when we are fed and ready we need to go back to sea.'

And this we did. Through signs and what words we could share I got to know the slaves and their origins, heard about their lands and families and this is how we learned to get on together.

Chapter 10

Carausius

After many more days at sea, we were approaching my home waters. Rowing in turns and using the ragged repaired sail in favourable winds the journey had passed uneventfully. We had rounded the great headland at the west of the land where many ship had foundered in storms and turned in a northerly direction. These were familiar waters, I knew them like the back of my hand. I wondered what I would find. Were my mother and father still well? And my brothers? How was the trading? And what would they think of my return with the strange bunch of dishevelled men? I then realised that I looked a sight too. My hair was long and matted and my beard which used to be neatly trimmed had gone wild. Would they even recognise me? I had been young, idealistic and clean-shaven when I left. My body had filled out and developed strong muscles, and I looked like the warrior that I had become. Much had happened in the four years that had now passed.

As we approached the harbour a commotion started as people gathered to see this strange ship approach. Used to trading vessels, this ship was obviously different. I saw old Llyr standing on the jetty. He was one thing that did not change. He treated me like a son, and I saw him as a father figure when my own was consumed by running his business. I loved his tolerance, patience and guidance as he taught me about ships and their habits.

We managed a passable performance of an arrival. We dropped the sail, gathered and furled what we could, and shipped oars as we glided to the jetty. Our ropes were taken and we slowly disembarked. Llyr looked at me, wondering what this apparition was. Then his withered old face broke out in a broad smile.

'Ceris, I thought I would never see you again.'

We embraced. Then he pushed away to study the ship.

'Is there anything you can't break?'

Our ungainly group of unkempt men walked through the town and the townsfolk came out to look. They gathered on street corners and as word spread they even came out from the inn. Two off-duty Roman soldiers stiffened in suspicion and one noticed that I was carrying my centurion's helmet and was wearing obvious but battered Roman uniform. He hesitated, then rose to his feet and saluted. This caused even more confusion in the minds of the townsfolk until there was a gradual recognition of who it was leading this strange band.

As we approached the great hall, we had acquired quite a group of followers. My father Caradog emerged to see what the fuss was about. He stood still until in surprise he recognised me despite my appearance. He stepped forward and took me in his arms.

'My son' he simply said. He stepped back. 'My Ceris, you have become a man.' As he took in my strange band, he asked 'Ceris, who are these people?

I said 'It's quite a story but they are with me and they have become my loyal friends.'

A voice from behind me asked 'Carausius?'

I turned to see Darius with a confused expression. 'What is this Ceris?'

It was my father's turn to be confused. I explained that my Romanised name was Carausius and that was how I was known to everyone outside this land. I would explain all later. My mother had appeared behind my father. There were tears in her eyes as she held me in her arms. For once in her life she was speechless. Her usually haughty demeanour cracked. I realised that having carried me, birthed me, fed me and cared for me while I grew just what I meant to her.

When she had regained her composure, she said 'I thought I would never see you again and now you have returned. Thanks be to all the gods and spirits.'

There was a moment when I almost lost my speech too. At the entrance to the hall appeared Anwen, the girl I had missed, my girl from the town that I had loved and dreamed about. She gave me a hesitant smile, obviously unsure of how I would react seeing her with my family. I could not help but return a broad smile of happiness, and was struck anew by her natural beauty. As I beamed at her, I was struck completely dumb by a movement behind her skirts. The fabric seemed to move of its own volition. I could not initially quite make sense of that and my mind seized up as the face of a little child of about three years of age peered shyly out from behind.

Anwen looked at me uncertainly as my mother said 'You didn't know about the leaving present you gave us. But never mind, we took your girl in, she had a fine healthy daughter and she is now part of the family.'

I dropped to my knees, and this beautiful little girl cautiously approached me. For the last few steps she ran into my arms.

I heard Anwen say softly 'Alys, this is your father, returned to us.'

I could not see for tears but stood and reached out for Anwen. We fell into an embrace and I picked up my Alys and we held her between us.

Chapter 11

Carausius

That night we feasted. How we feasted! I explained about my men, and how I had got to the present time through my adventures in Gaul. I told of the great storm, and as modestly as I could about how I had taken control of the stricken ship. I told of the slaves, shackled to the ship and at the mercy of the Romans and the forces of nature. My father had complained 'More mouths to feed' but I could see he did not mean it as heartfeltedly as he might. I explained that my freeing them had brought a loyalty and devotion that made me feel a responsibility for them, albeit one that made me uncomfortable, unworthy even. 'They are good men. Some come from lands in the eastern empire, taken in war and others have committed crimes, often in desperation, that got them a sentence of galley slave. Apart from their strength, some have skills in crafts, woodworking and some look as if they can fight. We can find a place for them and they will earn their keep. Llyr in the shipyard needs more help as our need for our trading ships has grown'.

Life settled down. I had to get used to having a daughter and being a father. I found her enchanting, curious and beautiful like her mother, and I was enthralled yet mystified by her. What have I produced, I asked myself in amazement. Before my mother could start dropping hints and looking at me in her critical or disappointed way (I knew her so well), I walked along the sea with Anwen and asked her to marry me. The sun was shining, the waves broke musically on the shore and it felt like paradise. I remembered her comment from years ago about her poor background and told her she was already part of the family and her demeanour was quite suitable for a royal role. She laughed at that and saw that I was teasing her and agreed to marry. I announced this at our family dinner and was cheered, toasted and told how lucky I was. On that day, she had never looked more beautiful. I thought she outshined the sun.

My brothers and I sailed on trading missions, selling what we had an excess of and buying what we needed or could sell on. Cloths, wines and oils, jewellery and trinkets, we sold them all. We traded in Menapia in the east of Ireland, and travelled to Gaul for wine. We prospered and our town grew rich. More trade, more visitors, more Romans. We had our entertainments, of course, from games to women. The Romans talked of amphitheatres, great arenas where games and competitions could be held. I knew of course of their savage side too. Wild animals and human warriors and even religious dissidents were offered for slaughter as a form of gruesome entertainments for the crowds. I wondered if we should construct one to attract more visitors and their money.

My slaves, or my men, as they had become, adapted to life in the town in different ways. Some were workers in the shipyard, some became crew members for our trading voyages and others found employment with local builders who were thriving with work and the newest techniques for building. Some relationships with women in the town developed, and there was a general feeling that this place had become their home.

Anwen thrived as a mother. I knew she was mine and we loved each other. The townsfolk accepted her rise in position. She had been one of them and still seen as one in many respects. Little Alys grew and became a confident leggy young girl, skipping around, asking questions and sometimes bewildering me with her insights or amusing me with her misinterpretations of things. If corrected she would put her head on one side, and look at me as if to say that she knew that really. Anwen became pregnant again. I secretly wondered if I would have a son, but knew from the joy of having Alys that whatever the baby was I would be happy. And happy life was, until one day when things changed.

Once again, Arthfael and his family were visiting, this time to celebrate the return of Xander. After four years he had returned looking like a young Roman official. I wondered what my uncle made of his son. He didn't fit in well before, and knowing the expression 'a fish out of water' he looked even more out of place. I had a moment of concern when I saw the way that Xander looked at Anwen. He had matured into a man and I did not like the lustful looks he gave her when she was not looking. Once I caught his eye and glared my disapproval. He turned away like a beaten dog. I had much in my life and he knew it and I saw his jealousy. My father and uncle seemed closer through the experience of having us taken away. Both were glad to have their sons restored to them. I think it was more straightforward for my father. He could see the son he used to have, albeit now influenced by his Roman experiences in the wider world. In his eyes I was now fully a man, yet very much of his family. Arthfael however I could see was confused. His quiet son seemed further away from his hopes and expectations. He had developed a degree of sophistication and carried himself as a full adult. He insisted on wearing his old togas, although they were getting stained and threadbare. I did overhear a conversation between our parents that surprised me. Xander, or Allectus as he insisted on being called had actually wrought a change in his dour and rigid father. My own was being his cheerful and positive self, prepared to fend off the predictable attitude of my uncle, but Arthfael said 'I know my son and I are different and I know you mean well when you offer me advice. I have been listening and that boy does have interesting ideas sometimes. He sat me down and told me to listen. He ordered me! I will tell you what he said and it makes sense'.

'Father, I have seen the workings of the empire in London. It does not just run on might; it depends on supplies and commerce. I've been thinking. You know the Augusta legion at Caerleon that you go on about so much?. Have you considered what a legion needs? It's not just five thousand soldiers, it's the officers, families, servants, slaves, blacksmiths, artisans.... Do you know how much effort goes into sourcing food, fabrics, metals? Even wines and oils. You are envious of the prosperity of uncle Caradog, I know. You may deny it but it is obvious. Wait and I will tell you of our opportunity. I can call on the commander and the quartermaster and offer to arrange supplies. I will take the burden off them. I know the workings so well I can give them a list of their requirements before they have a chance to think. We have farmers who grow crops and breed animals, and we can work with uncle Caradog on importing wines and olive oil from southern Gaul and around the great middle sea.'

'Well, Caradog, I thought this boy is talking sense. Rather than resenting the Romans, we will use them to make us wealthy. I'd never thought of things like that. He's already gathered some local businessmen and traders to get this going. He may not have much brawn but he has some brains, I must say.'

I was astonished to see and hear the changes in Xander since he had become Allectus in London. From his descriptions of his life there, it sounded like a holiday. While I had to do my ablutions in streams and behind bushes, and fight for my life, he was reaping the modern benefits of what Rome brought to our lands. Bathing, warm water, drying towels, no wonder it had turned his head. Instead of driving him further from his father, though, they seemed to have found a common purpose. That was good, I suppose, although how the primitive existence in Siluria would suit him in the longer term I do not know. It would be a while before he could build his own villa, I thought. After our experiences, I had learned about Roman ways of war and was glad to be home, but what our newly formed Allectus had learned in London had captured him for Rome and he seemed even more out of place here.

I was walking on the jetty with Llyr a few weeks later when I had saw what he had done to my Roman ship. The timbers were repaired, oars fashioned and she looked restored in her hull. But Llyr had fulfilled his earlier ambition. Instead of the squat mast and square sail, he had replaced it with a much taller one which now supported a larger twin boomed triangular sail such as he had made for his prototype dinghy.

'Are you ready to take her out?' he asked.

I needed no encouragement. There was a stiff breeze blowing so this would be a good test of her capabilities. Calling to Darius, he gathered eight of what I now thought of as my men, and we clambered aboard. With Darius and I standing on the stern deck, I steered while the men rowed us away from the jetty. We untied and raised the sail as I positioned the ship across the wind. She stiffened, leaned and accelerated as the men cheered. I headed her up cautiously towards the wind, and while she slowed, she confirmed to me that this sailing rig could do what we had heard and move us towards it. Looking at landmarks on the shore, I also saw that we were not following a straight course but losing ground by going side-ways as well. I thought about this as we learned to manoeuvre the sail by tacking through the wind and realised that the boat needed resistance to reduce this. On our return to shore I discussed this with Llyr and we came up with the idea of deepening the keel. A further plank of timber was shaped and attached, and on testing this indeed reduced the side-ways motion.

A few weeks later I had gone to the shipyard to inspect the repairs to one of our trading ships that had received some damage in a storm, but was distracted to see that my ship was not at the jetty. Hearing distant shouts I looked around and at sea I saw Darius at the helm of my ship, the men cheering as he was clearly in control of all that was going on. He supervised the dropping and furling of the sail and brought the ship into the jetty under oars, which were shipped neatly. He jumped off the ship and came up to me laughing.

'You can sail?' I said in surprise.

'Yes, I have watched everything you have done, and now I can sail like', he hesitated, 'a duck.'

'A duck?' I queried.

'Well, maybe a fish. Anyway you are a good teacher without knowing it.'

I felt admiration for these men, so far from their lands, making the most of life and revealing such a range of skills.

Chapter 12

Quintus

I have been summoned again to attend the court of Maximian. I note the word. I knew it, I just knew it! In far off lands, Diocletian has defeated emperor Carinus and claimed the whole of the empire in his name. He had now installed Maximian as his Caesar. I knew the two of them had ambition, now it is revealed. As usual I ask myself why I am summoned and examine my actions. I cannot see anything that might have caused his displeasure, so I set off from London with six of my soldiers to take ship from Dover. The crossing is miserable, as usual. The sea is unhappy, the boat restless. Each breaking and curling wave beckons to my stomach. I am certainly a land creature, I think and am glad when we reach Boulogne. We spend the night at the great fort and find horses, load up our belongings and set off. Passing through Gaul, I note that it feels peaceful. No men can be seen to bear arms and a few peasants gaze sullenly as we pass, but I feel no threat. My escorts surround me and as we ride, my thoughts turn to Maximian. What now does he want? He has land, wealth and a reputation. Perhaps that is not enough. He may want more. A war leader and an army get restless with nothing to do. His council advise and rule in his name. Soldiers at peace become bored and listless. With no chance of plunder, morale falls. Polishing and parading is fine before battle, it strengthens the spirits. At peace it becomes repetitive and dull. Emperors have been deposed for lack of ambition as well as failure.

Maybe he wants a war. My thoughts broaden. Where might he go next? Into the colder northern regions? To Ireland, reputed to be green and fertile but with more savages to fight? What could he gain? They continue to raid and at times the Welsh and the Romans have cooperated and fought together to keep them off Welsh soil and by and large that situation is managed. And Caledonia, north of the walls built to keep them from raiding England? I have seen the great wall of Hadrian, flowing across the landscape like a stone ribbon. A bleak place to be stationed, I thought and there were many forts along its length to be garrisoned. The wall kept the peace but memories of the defeat a hundred years ago under the emperor Septimius Severus whose desire for an imperial triumph overrode others warnings. Finally, when goaded by the northerners, the famed IX Hispana legion was drawn first to invade, then led further and further north into unfamiliar terrain by an enemy that refused battle. Somewhere in the dark forests the entire legion was slaughtered, never to be seen again. Such was the shame of this loss which included their legionary Eagle they were remembered only by silence. This large number of Roman deaths surely offered a strong warning to Maximian about repeating such an adventure.

Arriving at the palace he has claimed with his new status I walked through the gardens, landscaped and manicured, into the hall with murals and mosaics. I marvelled at the expense lavished on this. He has just had a son who was called Maxentius; perhaps he might be less ambitious and more willing to live with what he had achieved. Representatives of the great western empire gathered. We took refreshments and talked as old friends. I could find no source of tension or argument as we waited for Maximian and his council to convene the meeting.

He saw me and said 'Quintus, I am pleased to see you. I thought you had perished in the great storm. We lost a few ships those days, I can tell you.'

I thanked him for his concern without wasting words as he could see I was alive. As the meeting progressed I duly made my report which confirmed that taxes were paid on time and tributes, slaves and hostages were collected. The mood was calm as yet more reports were made from other regions. Maximian then voiced the reason for calling us together.

'I thank you for your reports. I can see no reason to be dissatisfied with any of you, but here is one problem we must address. While Gaul is at peace and has accepted Roman rule, this will not last while we have raiders and pirates coming down the sea from the north. They steal and burn and carry off people as slaves. They are attacking the southern and eastern parts of Britain too. As we have made these lands part of our empire, it follows that if we cannot protect them, they will start to doubt our power and they will not accept our rule.'

He outlined the problem of these small raiding ships, often attacking at night, with quick savage assaults on small coastal towns, villas and estates.

'We have a great fleet, with ships at Boulogne and Dover, but they cannot set to sea quickly, they depend on many oarsmen, and to get the crew of sailors and soldiers assembled takes time. We cannot leave the ships on alert continuously. We get some warnings from our fishing boats some of the time but otherwise we are in the dark. Another problem is that the pirates use the shallows of a coastline they know well and can duck into estuaries and creeks to escape. They can hide for days if they want to. Our most powerful ships cannot be used like this.'

He hesitated, not someone used to seeking advice on military matters. 'Does anyone have any suggestions?'

I looked at the people around me. I was a military man through and through. I did not think that the silver-tongued administrators and politicians would have much to offer. I doubted if some of them could tell one end of a ship from the other. A silence fell as no-one had anything to say. Maximian's expression was one of frustration and growing anger. Why have all these advisers if they had nothing to advise?

I rose to my feet. 'Your excellency, you have outlined the problem well and explained our difficulties in countering this.'

Start with flattery and take courage, I told myself.

'What we need are faster small heavily armed ships, with a commander who is skilled with sailing and knows these waters and how to cope with the challenges they give. With well trained crews I believe these pirates can be tamed.'

I sat down. A few murmurs came from the rest, although I thought I was stating the obvious. Maximian replied 'Well that's as may be but we are no further on. Continue.'

That's me on the spot, I told myself. I rose to my feet again.

'We need a strategy and the tactics will follow. We also need to think widely. We have agreed that we do not have the right ships, we do not have commanders with skills in these waters or the knowledge of their dangers. In the great Middle Sea there are storms like anywhere else, but there are not great tides that can outrun a ship, or sandbanks or mudbanks to catch them. Good as our commanders are, we should accept that they may not be the best.'

Maximian bristled as I criticised his fleet so I hesitated until he said 'Carry on, let me hear more of your ideas; no-one else has anything to offer.'

I continued 'A year ago, as you know, I was caught in the great storm. It was clear that our captain could not cope and I was convinced that the ship was lost. I was making peace with my gods when he was washed overboard. I thought my time was up, but you remember that young Welshman I brought to fight in your army?'

I felt I was taking ownership of this plan so might as well claim some credit.

'Carausius fought bravely for Rome and you were kind enough to compliment him and allow him to return to his home.'

He said 'I do remember him well. He became rather popular, I thought.'

I suddenly realised that Maximian had been disquieted by this and allowing his return was not a magnanimous act. Bringing him back into our service might be dangerous for me. After a short silence, he said again 'Carry on.'

Still standing, I said 'That young man saved the ship, he saved my life and the lives of my men. He is more at home on a ship than on the land; he says the sea is in his blood. He took control and the ship seemed to obey him and the crew followed. My suggestion is that he more than anyone has the ability to take on this problem. I know he is not of Rome, but if he should fail, that would not be to the detriment of Rome's reputation.'

I thought my last comment showed a rare bit of political skill. We could disown him if necessary and keep our, or rather Maximian's hands clean.

He looked thoughtful.'There may be much in your idea that is good. I will think on it, and as Britain is your province hold you responsible.'

I realised I was caught in a trap. From trying to impress him with my plan, which I thought was sound and better than anything else (not that was any practical alternative), I was now embroiled in it. If it proceeded, I was to be held responsible. If it succeeded I may be allowed some credit, but if it failed, I would go down with the ship, I thought wryly, or end up wishing I had. Next morning, Maximian joined me, clapped his arm around my shoulder and handed me a codicil bearing Carausius's appointment as commander of the fleet of Rome in Britain.

'You know what to do' he said in his quietly threatening way, 'just don't fail me.'

So once again I took ship to Britain, crossing the great channel and with my escort taking horses to travel across to this strange kingdom of the west where the Welsh and the Romans actually seemed capable of working together. We stayed in the now familiar chain of forts and as I rode I reflected on how my life and very existence had become so tied up with these people.

Chapter 13

Carausius

My father was walking through the town inspecting the progress of the new buildings when the atmosphere changed. A feeling of something in the air, he said later. A hush fell as a group of Romans on horseback could be seen descending into the town. This was not the usual informality of visitors; this group seemed organised, a leader in front and two paired ranks of horsemen behind. As they got closer, he recognised Quintus and his escort and wondered what he wanted now. Quintus rode up and without dismounting raised a hand in greeting.

'Welcome' said my father in response 'would you and your men like some refreshments at my hall?'

'It's not you I want today' Quintus replied sharply, 'where is your son Carausius? I have a message.'

My father, biting back the instinct to say I was called Ceris, said that I was at the ship-yard, and Quintus, leaving his men, rode down and came towards me. As he approached, he swung himself off his horse and dropped the reins.

'Carausius' he said curtly.

I was surprised to see him and asked what I could do for him and his face took on a serious expression.

'You will remember that the emperor reserved the right to call on you if he wanted?'

I felt a cold chill run through me. My life was good, I had a family who depended on me and I was of use to my father. I also had another child on the way.

'What could he possibly want of me now? I have served Rome well and I am settled here with my lands and my family.'

'Maximian has a problem and he thinks you can help him with it,' replied Quintus.

'What could I possibly have to offer that he could not get elsewhere?'

Quintus proceeded to describe the pirate raids that seemed impossible to stop. 'They come from the north, often at night. We don't know where they will strike next and Maximian takes this as a personal affront. It undermines his authority and loses respect for his rulership over these lands.'

'But why me?' I asked.

Quintus said firmly 'We have had to recognise that we do not have the right ships or experienced captains. I had the honour of describing your great skill in the storm to Maximian and I even admitted that you had saved my life. We have considered all options and we need someone with special talents. The description of the person we need is that he is a leader, he is brave, he can sail a ship and he can fight. That fits you, and I have to tell you that you are the only applicant.'

'Applicant?' I said, 'you seem to think that I want this.'

He replied 'What Maximian wants, Maximian gets.'

I said angrily 'And it sounds as if you are responsible for my plight.'

He handed me the codicil of appointment. I looked at it in amazement. I had been appointed as commander in chief of the entire Roman fleet in Britain and Gaul. I realised that the full responsibility of this task was mine and mine alone. Was I really the only person they thought could deal with these pirates? I considered refusing, but knowing Maximian and the revenge he could unleash on our stable lands and destroy all that my family had built, realised that I could not. Despite my forebodings, I started to consider how I might achieve this, and how ship to ship combat in small ships could be made effective.

There was great distress within the family at my recall to the service of Maximian. I had told them of his nature and brutality. There was fear for my life and uncertainty at how long I would be away. What if I did not come back? I had described the nature of my call-back and what I would have to do. My responsibilities had grown. When I had been called away nearly ten years ago, I did not return for nearly four. I was now nearly thirty years old, and while I felt as fit as I had in those fighting days, my body bothered me with more aches and pains these days. I prepared to leave, and as word got around people looked at me with sympathy. Anwen was of course the most worried. I heard her trying to explain to Alys that Daddy was having to go away again. Alys went quiet and then I heard her saying the she would be very good and help with the new baby when it came. Her solemn little voice nearly reduced me to tears. Leaving them was by far the worst part.

Putting these feelings aside, I decided to sail around to Dover rather than travel on horseback. The more I thought about the ships that the pirates were likely to use, the more I thought I could use mine to defeat them. She had manoeuvrability, could sail better than any other ship of her size and point upwind to be less dependent on rowers, who I might need as fighters too. What's more I loved her and had made her mine as she had saved my life with her seaworthiness. I went to the harbour to tell Llyr that I needed my ship preparing. I had a list of spares and would have liked to take another sail but space was limited as we had to carry weapons as well. I had my Roman uniform washed and my helmet polished and its plume of authority brushed.

As I arrived, I was heartened to find Darius and my men lined up as if coming with me was the most natural thing they could think of. There are no people I would have preferred although I did not know if they would go to war for Rome, knowing how she had treated them. I already had a few volunteers from the town looking for adventure, if not fame or fortune. I thanked them, offered them a chance to stay where they were settled, but none wanted that. I was humbled by their loyalty and offered my gratitude. I selected the strongest looking so we had a full complement of oarsmen.

The day of our departure came. Most of the town turned out to wave us off. Adventure by proxy for some, I thought, but I knew their gesture stemmed from their loyalty to my family. My parents and Anwen and Alys came to the quayside. Anwen was heavily pregnant now and I saw how she was holding back her tears. I whispered my pride in her and how much I loved her.

'Farewell, my princess, but I will see you all again soon,' I said, though we both knew that some things are unanswerable. Suddenly, from behind the body of the crowd appeared Allectus. I was surprised that he would travel so far to make an effort to see us off, but more so when he appealed 'Take me with you.'

I looked at him. 'We are going into danger here and you are neither a warrior nor a sailor.'

He said 'I will make myself useful; you know how I don't fit in here. I am slowly dying in our world having seen another one.'

'What will my uncle say if I take you away?'

'I have set him up to become rich. My best merchants are now dealing with the Romans so I have done what I said I would. Besides I am a man and must make my own decisions' he paused, drawing himself up to his full height 'and mistakes.'

I thought for a moment and said 'You will need some decent clothes!'

We cast off, and with me at the helm, rowed out of the harbour and into the sea. The conditions were favourable so we hoisted the sail and gradually disappeared from sight of my home. We crossed the sea to the rocky south-west corner of Britain with ease, sailing by day and night. As we rounded the great headland, Darius was on the helm and I was impressed by his feel for the boat. He made corrections of course instinctively and once the coast was more favourable to us, we stopped in coves or small harbours for more comfortable nights and to pick up supplies. Some of the people in the towns looked at us with concern as we had a military air about us, while others came close to look at our sail. With the southeast winds of the season behind us, we made good progress towards Dover. We passed on the seaward side of the island the Romans called Vectis so I could, without warning, expose my crew to some rather choppy seas off the southernmost cape. I wondered if I could make Allectus sick. He couldn't have looked less like a sailor. I felt a pang of guilt for being cruel. However, all passed without difficulty and we continued on our way.

Finally we approached the great harbour at Dover. The hilltop castle and great lighthouse could be seen from miles away, and slowly we started to see some large ships tied up on jetties. If this represented the power of Rome, it seemed mighty and impregnable to me. As we closed, we took down our sail, securing it while the rowers deployed their oars. I wanted to tell them to coordinate their rowing, and ship their oars together when I ordered but I held back as I knew in my heart that they wanted to be as skilled in their arrival as I did.

We coasted into a space on a jetty in a fine manner. Nothing to embarrass or shame us here, I thought. As we secured the ship, a senior officer approached in his uniformed finery, with a group of attendants behind him. He greeted me formally.

'I am Gaius Iulius Marcellus, commander of the Roman port and fortress of Dover.'

I returned his salute saying 'I am...'

He interrupted 'I well know who you are, your reputation precedes you. You are welcome and I can even tell you some of your old friends are here.'

Two soldiers who were hovering in the background caught my eye, and to my discomfort saluted casually and shouted 'Hail Carausius.'

Marcellus studied my ship. 'Isn't that one of ours?'

I answered 'It was. You will see that some modifications to improve it have been made.'

'Yes it looks quite different.'

He then looked at my men who were disembarking and looking around uncertainly.

'They are our slaves, aren't they?'

'Slaves no longer,' I said, 'I have freed them.'

'By whose authority?' he asked.

'Mine' I replied, looking at him straight in the eye. 'This one is Darius, he sails like a duck.'

Marcellus raised an eyebrow and was about to speak.

'Don't ask,' I said.

Allectus was standing nearby and I was amused to see that he had slipped on a toga that he had brought in his belongings.

I introduced my cousin, and Marcellus said 'You are welcome too. I will have you shown to your quarters to freshen yourselves up and we will dine tonight. I have been told to give you absolute authority over the pirate matter and you can explain your plans and strategy over dinner tonight. I am sure you have lots of stories to tell as well. I will have the slaves,' he hesitated, 'your men, taken care of in the barracks. They will be treated well.'

That night we dined with Marcellus in the officers' quarters, which were in a fine stone building in the grounds of the great cliff-top castle. Lit by torches, with the walls draped by flags and banners, I felt their history was on display. A group of his officers, both naval and army, and various port officials were present and the atmosphere was formal. Allectus and I were tired but did our best to remain alert. Very few had met me before and my reputation was perhaps sullied in their eyes by my being an outsider in terms of Roman citizenship. I sensed from the beginning a few undercurrents of discontent. There was a feeling of resentment from some of the naval people. I think they had picked up on the idea that Maximian thought they were not up to the task of defeating the pirates, and saw my appointment as commander as undermining the authority of Marcellus, but he behaved well and gave no hint or sign that he felt this was a problem. Perhaps, like Quintus, he felt that a degree of distance from my actions might give a political advantage if I gave rise to the emperor's disapproval. I wondered if I was being unfair on the man as his general helpful disposition gave the lie to my suspicions. The army leaders were different. I sensed that my military history made them feel I was one of them and knew more about the reality of their lives and work than the naval side. Much of the conversations stemmed from the recent campaigns, and we shared our stories and even, when the evening relaxed, joked and laughed about some of the situations our fellow soldiers had got themselves into.

I avoided getting drawn into discussing or sharing my plans for my campaign. I wanted time to study the resources I had before I could work out what I needed. I was pleased to see Allectus involved in discussions with some of the officials and learned later that he had been talking about funds, budgets and things of which I had little interest but clearly would need to know about in my planning. Uncertainty about bringing him changed to an appreciation that he could be a real help. At the end of the evening I had learned about the command structure of the base and who did what in its running. I had made a judgment about which officers I could count on and who might be unhelpful or obstructive.

Allectus and I repaired to our rooms in the officers' mess and agreed to meet in the morning for a joint inspection of the fort and naval base. Looking at things from different perspectives with different eyes was valuable and made me feel for the first time that I was lucky to have him with me, even if we were somewhat uneasy with each other.

Chapter 14

Carausius

After a hearty breakfast we were ready to explore our new home. We had seen much of the castle so we walked down to the great harbour. I was keen not to have an entourage trailing behind so we walked quickly and purposefully down the road to the main jetties. We studied the sheer size of the mighty biremes and triremes with their banks of oars and calculated the number of crew needed from the oarsmen to the military contingent, who I had learned were called marine soldiers, often abbreviated to just marines. They were large enough to carry a considerable amount of weaponry to use against enemies and the ship itself was equipped with a large ram clad in bronze on the waterline at the bow. I imagined the damage that would do to the planking of any ship that was in its way and the panic as water poured in. All this, however, served to confirm my thoughts that these ships were too large and unwieldy to use against smaller pirate ships which I needed to learn more about. As we moved onto the boatyard against whose smaller jetty my ship was secured, I did think of one feature of these ships that we could use. I admired the size of the channels in which several ships were being built before being hauled down to the sea for launch, and thought wistfully of old Llyr at home. He would like to see this, I thought. His constructions were miracles wrought from more basic facilities. The team of shipwrights was led by a weather-beaten old man from the same mould as my old Llyr. Perhaps they are from a standard design, I wondered. He was proud of his skills and showed me around the workshop with its range of tools for sawing, chopping, shaping and cutting. All reflected the scale of the enterprise here and things were clearly run efficiently, and I made my plans to build my new fleet.

I tried to find witnesses who had seen the sort of ships the pirates used. The most useful were the fishermen who lived around the edges of the port. If they were seen by the pirates, their ships were small and of no consequence or threat so left alone. Their eyes though saw and remembered, and two fishermen described vessels of similar size to mine, bulkier in shape and with perhaps a dozen oars and the usual square sail on a short mast. With this information I could start to calculate how I would get to attack them.

We returned to the main jetty under the towering lighthouse. I again marvelled at the sheer size of some of the stones that built it and wondered how it had been done. Allectus just said that the buildings in London were bigger and more impressive still, so I decided to say nothing. Several groups of soldiers were sitting around and they got to their feet as I approached. Again I got a 'Hail Carausius' and thought that this was becoming a bit of an embarrassing joke, but I was also aware that the response was ragged and I realised that there was a lack of purpose about these men. Perhaps they need encouragement and the prospect of action to restore their self-respect, I thought.

Marcellus found us later and I started to explain my wishes.

'I need your boatyard to make me two more ships

using mine as an example. I am going to show you how well she sails and that she can out-manoeuvre a pirate ship.'

Marcellus looked sceptical so I said 'I am going to arrange a demonstration. Tomorrow you, your senior officers and some of the boatyard crew are going to sea.'

Marcellus asked 'Is that an order?'

I raised an eyebrow. 'What do you think?'

He left to act on this and select his people. I said to Allectus quietly 'To get them supportive of this we must make them feel confident in my planning. Can you speak to the old ship-wright and make a list of all you will need to build these ships speedily. I'm not going to wait for anyone else to create delays or obstacles.'

Allectus smiled and went off to do what he was good at. I went to find Darius who was going to play a key part in my efforts to build a functioning team.

The next morning was fine, with a steady breeze. I borrowed a small rowing boat and went out to place some weighted buoys in the harbour. As the officers gathered, a couple of boatyard workers joined us, trying not to be overwhelmed by the amount of naval authority.

I addressed them. 'Today you will see what this one ship can do. You will act as equal members of the crew and obey my captain. I hope you enjoy the experience.'

Darius appeared on deck, exuding his usual air of serenity and dignity, and beckoned his new crew aboard. A few of his stronger oarsmen were in place but some of the gaps needing filling. There was some disquiet as they realised that I was leaving them to the care of this man who had a few years ago been their slave. However, to their credit, and perhaps in deference to my great authority, they obediently climbed on board and Darius allocated their roles. They cast off, and rowed out until they could pull up the great sail. For the next few hours they sailed in and outside the harbour, at different aspects to the wind, and around the marker buoys that I had put out earlier.

While they were doing this, and I hoped enjoying the experience, I went to find the captain of the marine soldiers. He turned out to be one of Maximian's veterans called Tertius, a no-nonsense man I warmed to. We had campaigned together in Gaul, in different sections of the legion, and he was interested to hear what I proposed.

'When we have the three ships we are going pirate hunting. I want you to lead the training because the sailors will be controlling the ships and I need your marines to provide the force. Boarding ships in moving seas is difficult, and one missed footing can mean going overboard and with armour there is nothing you can do to avoid drowning. I don't want to lose men unnecessarily and we will have to wait to find out how the pirates fight.'

He looked pleased to have something to plan for and a new challenge.

I added 'Training will help us choose the best marines for the job.'

I left with the feeling that he was on my side for this campaign.

Back on the jetty I waited as the ship returned. I noted a spring in the steps of the crew that disembarked that was more than just a welcome return to solid land. I heard comments that said they were impressed at what my ship could do, and they had all played a part in learning this. I could even think that they had enjoyed being ordered about. I didn't think that any had been on such a pleasure cruise before.

Marcellus said 'I can actually now believe that you can catch some of these pirates. I had my doubts but no answers before.'

I replied 'I hope so. I need more ships like this and have made arrangements with the boatyard for the construction of two more'.

Marcellus stiffened 'We will have to organise..'

I interrupted 'Allectus has met with your ship-wright, two of his men sailed with you today and orders are being placed. My men have boatbuilding experience from my home and I expect things will proceed smoothly.'

It did go smoothly though it took longer than I hope, taking, six months until the second of the new ships was completed. Sourcing the long timbers for the keel and the spars required delivery from many miles away. Ship building over the years had exhausted nearer supplies, and each tree had to be inspected for disease and shape before it was felled. Dragged by strong horses, we slowly build up materials and the keels were laid in two of the larger channels in the shoreline. Allectus had seized the purse strings and a fair price was paid for everything. Ropes were made, fabric was woven, nails were forged and slowly my ships took shape. While contemplating the features of a trireme I had noticed the boarding platforms built on the sides of the hull. These also offered protection to the oars which could be smashed in collisions and I thought that widening the gunwales of our ships to provide firmer footing for our boarding parties would be a good idea that would also offer some protection to the oars if they were trailing in the water. I had my ship rowed around to the yard and these modifications made.

We were now ready for training. I had commandeered a cross-channel cargo ship of the right size and hull shape to represent a pirate ship. Tertius produced a dozen fit men who seemed enthusiastic about the prospect of some sort of action to relieve the monotony of port duties. Tertius in his gruff way addressed them and told them he was going to work them hard to stop them getting wet and drowning in the service of the emperor. He introduced me formally although I was by now well-known to them. I explained that we would be practising boarding ships and it was different from attacking a rampart on land whether muddy or not.

'Tertius has given you the general idea, and you have

all been on ships, but I remind you that they move from side to side, and end to end and can have very slippery decks and bits to trip over. We may be attacking in the dark so you need to know your way around the ship too. Mistakes mean you die. Even if you swim well, your armour will take you down. Even if we can see you, we will not be able to help you.'

Having divided the marines into two groups of six, I took out the first on my ship. They were lightly dressed and un-armed. As we approached the cargo ship, they prepared the iron grappling hooks I had had made. The sea was slight but there was still enough movement to make jumping from one to the other require some judgement, and as the first three threw their hooks, I saw some hesitancy in one. He slipped and almost went over the side. The other two landed on the deck of our prey, and the second three followed swiftly.

Over the next weeks I rehearsed both teams in all sorts of weather, and as their confidence grew, started them carrying weapons, which reduced their ability to hang on, and nervously for us all, wearing light armour. I installed short ropes attached to bags of horsehair and rushes to the hull to be thrown if we saw someone fall in. I knew these would help them float for a while but they were for mental support as much as anything; I needed them to feel confident. Their initial nervousness had been marked by anxious laughter and scathing comments about those who slipped or fell. These attacks were now carried out with quiet efficiency. I knew the teams were bonding with the self-confidence and trust that was needed in a fighting unit and felt they were ready for our task.

The second of my ships was now ready. I had a message from Quintus saying that Maximian was getting impatient as the raiders were behaving with impunity. I did not need telling of Maximian's nature, and replied with a short note saying we were about to start our campaign. There was one final task of preparation. Marcellus looked on in confusion as both ships were pulled onto the shore and stripped of their sails. The hulls were darkened with pitch, and the sails dyed dark blue in large vats. Once everything was dry, they were relaunched, and the sails re-hung. I said to Marcellus that we were ready.

'We will be attacking at night and these are my nighthawks.' And to my men 'We are going to war. You are the best and we are ready.'

Chapter 15

Pirates

It was dusk as the ship arrived. It was rowed silently up the river to the small town in northern Gaul. The small sail was secured tightly to the mast. The moon was starting to rise, the birds were quiet and the townsfolk were starting to settle in their homes of stones and thatch after a day of toil. A fine Roman villa sat nearby, and light from oil lamps leaked from the windows. Its grounds were separate but its walls were low and offered no obstacle. The crew of Saxon barbarians were well-versed in their raiding, and as the shadow of their ship passed through those cast by overhanging trees, they prepared to land. One group led by the leader made for the villa, the others waited by the huts. Dressed in dark furs, daubed with pigments and carrying axes and spears they would cast fear into anyone. The unsuspecting village lay silently until the sound of axes smashing into the doors of the villa shattered the calm of the night. Horses whinnied and dogs started to bark. The owner of the villa started to shout for help but was swiftly cut down by the axe of the leader. While the rest started to ransack it, the leader seized the wife and two children. A knife to the throat of the youngest stopped the woman from resisting. Her screams turned to sobs as she realised what was happening. At the same time, the other raiders were breaking into the huts. More screams followed and those who took up weapons were killed. The survivors were rounded up and made to stand in the centre of the village. Mostly women and children, the pirates assessed their worth, mostly in terms of attractiveness. Children could be used as slaves or brought up to be Saxon. Anything that could be taken as plunder was piled in the square. Metal cooking pots, tools and weapons were taken from the huts, but the villa yielded furs, jewellery and decorations in addition. Several younger women, including the wife of the villa owner, had their hands bound behind them. Many cried when they realised that they were being taken, and were helpless as their children clung to them. The wife of the villa owner maintained a quiet dignity, but even she gasped as the leader cut the throats of those deemed to have no value. The thatched roofs were set alight with torches, and a raider gestured towards the villa. The leader said 'No, leave it. It is a good building and someone will return. Then, so shall we'.

The loot and the prisoners were taken to the ship. The prisoners were pushed into the bilges, gagged and secured there. The crew pushed the ship from the shore, and with a falling tide rowed gently to the sea. By the light of the moon, they navigated the twists and turns into deeper water. There was a breeze blowing but the direction was unfavourable so the rowers continued to propel the ship as it turned north. The ship settled into a gentle rhythm and the raiders were somnolent and relaxed after another successful raid. There was little to stop them, after all.

Apart from the helmsman, staring intently ahead as he maintained his course home, there was no-one to see the two darkened ships gaining on them from astern. Silently they caught up, then when about to overhaul the raiders' vessel they turned alongside, hooks were thrown and before they could react, darkly-dressed armed men were on their decks, cutting down any raider who dared to resist. The leader bellowed and charged at the first of the boarders. Carausius stepped aside quickly and with one thrust of his gladius, sliced open the throat of the Saxon. Blood covered the deck and pulsed into the bilges. Resistance weakened at the loss of their leader and a few tried to surrender. Carausius knew of the savagery meted out by these raiders so showed no mercy. The remainder of the crew were cut down and their bodies thrown overboard. Carausius's men transferred the loot to the nighthawks and surveyed the captives. He saw the anxiety in their eyes and heard the crying of the children. He told them they were safe and would be taken to Britain, before being given transport across the channel back to Gaul. I am not a nursemaid, Marcellus can sort this out, he thought. When they were safely aboard, an axe in the bilges saw the raiders' ship sink below the waves.

His ships returned to Dover to be greeted with interest. He handed over the women and children and congratulated his men. Apart from a few cuts and bruises there was no loss to them. He put Allectus in charge of cataloguing and arranging storage of the plundered goods. Over the next months, many more raiders came as the weather improved. The third ship was completed and crewed by sailors from the navy chosen by Marcellus. He had trained them well, and the sailors and marines were well-versed in their tactics. Few raiders escaped. On one hand, those who got away would tell of these dark ships that would appear out of the night, without warning, to slaughter the crews and seize their spoils. On the other, the value of what he captured grew, and that generated money he could use. He tried to have one ship at sea in the approximate area of attack at any time. The area at risk was large and covered both sides of the channel. He sought information about possible sightings from the fishermen who were often out at night and developed a system of signals. He led many attacks himself and Darius proved an able captain too. He later ordered that the ships be captured where possible and brought to Dover where he could sell them to traders if undamaged.

Allectus took charge of the accounts and recorded the buying and selling of goods and captured ships. Carausius took it upon himself to increase the wages of the soldiers and sailors. Allectus had recognised that the cost of living was increasing and they were becoming worried and restless. With this and the excitement of their task, spirits were high and morale was strong for all.

Quintus came to Dover to find out what was going on and prepare a report for Maximian.

'You seem to be doing well.' was his first comment.

Carausius replied 'My ships and my strategy have delivered what I hoped. You can tell Maximian that, and perhaps he will let me go'.

Quintus said cautiously 'I will do that. While he needs you to succeed as you are doing, he is not pleased about anyone becoming too popular. Once he has used you he will be keen to see the back of you. You should not expect a medal.'

Chapter 16

Maximian

At his court Maximian is anxious. Now promoted yet again to Augustus as co-emperor to Diocletian, he bears total responsibility for the Western Roman Empire. Reports of raids have diminished but few details have been given to him. He has reason to feel satisfied or is it no reason to feel dissatisfied? He has summoned his council for its regular meeting and is waiting impatiently to hear from his British envoy Quintus. After the usual round of reports, he turns to Quintus.

'Let us hear of your idea for dealing with the pirates.'

Quintus notes that he is still held responsible and stands to address the council.

'I am pleased to report that pirate activity has dropped since my recommendation to put our man from Wales in charge. He has proved himself again and again, from the design of his ships to his fighting strategy. He has built a fine team of sailors and soldiers, trained them and had virtually no losses. Morale at Dover is high and there is a sense of pride that they are getting rid of the raiders. Citizens captured and rescued have been returned to Gaul and will tell of how we are dealing with this.'

He hesitates, knowing the sensitivities that Maximian bears.

'Your Excellency, Carausius' popularity surprises me, and now we have the experience and means to carry on our attacks, I wonder if the time has come to thank him and let him return to his homelands.'

Maximian thinks and replies 'As things are going well, we will keep him a while longer. Whatever we all think, the problem is still present.'

He turns to his council. 'Do we all agree?'

At this, another man, tall, and pale with a narrow face stands as if to speak. Maximian says 'Constantius, you have something to say?'

I can't quite believe it. Constantius is another from this military grouping that they all come from. Comrades in arms indeed, they are all hard fighting men. Streets away from the patrician families of old Rome where breeding was the key, they had risen from humble beginnings away from Rome itself and taken power. Between them, they now held the empire of Rome. It would not surprise me if Constantius is on the same path. Like the aristocrats of old, they join and entangle their families so that loyalties are built. I hear that he has set aside his wife, the mother of his son, Constantine, in order to marry a daughter of Maximian. How greedy must one be to behave like that? He briefly thinks, why not me too? Would I be capable of that? Could I take a great office? He answers his own thoughts, as he already knows. It is that I have no appetite for power like this. Constantly aware of rivals, eyeing up weaknesses, making alliances and scheming. I have enough to do with enemies in front of me.

His attention returns to Constantius who nods, 'I do. We must congratulate Quintus on his victories. He has done well and I must confess I had my doubts about bringing in an outsider. He does sound a remarkable man.' He smiles slyly 'I hear that a lot of goods and even ships are being captured. Perhaps Quintus could tell us of how our riches are growing?'

Quintus looks shocked and has no answer.

Constantius carries on 'It may be that this Carausius is becoming rich on this enterprise. Perhaps the money we need to maintain our empire is not as much as it might be, and the riches of our treasury are not growing. From what I hear of his popularity he may need wealth to fund some ambition that we are unaware of.'

Quintus, knowing his fate is tied up with this, starts to bluster. 'I know he desires only to return to his homeland; he has spoken of nothing else. He has served Rome as you required and acquitted himself well on both times we have demanded it.

Maximian is looking wary. Quintus is aware that Maximian's paranoia is never far beneath the surface. Risen from nothing he guards his power closely, knowing that others could be looking to depose him. In recent times the careers of many emperors have been short-lived. If times are hard and a rival offers more and is popular...

'I will not tolerate this. Quintus, you and the port commander Marcellus should have been watching for this possibility. I see how he could be scheming against me. Can I trust even you? I have always mistrusted his popularity. I think you may have been taken in by him, Quintus. Well, he's your creation. I order you to arrest him and bring him to me for questioning. The penalty for embezzlement is death and if he resists arrest, you are to kill him there and then. Do not fail me or you will suffer the same fate.'

Quintus, reeling from his change of fortune, leaves the court. He gathers his escort and sets out to return to Britain, knowing that his target will still be at the port of his arrival. He returns to Boulogne and awaits the next transport. A day is spent on the crossing, which mercifully was calm, and finally the ship docks at the jetty. Before he disembarks, he dons his uniform and helmet, and with his escort behind him, marches to find Carausius, who is standing and talking to Marcellus. Carausius starts to smile but stops when he sees the expression on Quintus face and the tightly ordered group of soldiers behind him.

'I am ordered to arrest you and take you to Maximian.'

'For what reason?' asks Carausius.

'The charge is embezzlement of funds due to the Roman treasury. Maximian is wondering where the proceeds of your Saxon adventures have gone. He does not like the thought of you getting rich at what he sees as his expense.'

'I assure you that I have not benefitted. Some goods are stored, and from selling some boats I have restored the salaries of the troops here.' replies Carausius.

Watching this exchange, several groups of sailors and soldiers start to move within earshot. Some murmuring is heard, and Marcellus moves away to discourage the growing throng.

Quintus says 'You are coming with me. This is serious; the sentence for embezzlement is death.'

He turns to his soldiers. 'Arrest him.'

They hesitate. 'I do not wish to repeat this order.' he says angrily.

Still, the soldiers do not move. The murmuring in the background turns to shouts. 'Leave him.' 'No, you must not take him.' At this stand-off Quintus is clearly both annoyed and confused. No orders of his have been refused before, and he felt he carried the loyalty of his escort and that has now been challenged.

He glares at Carausius. 'I order you to come with me now on that ship.'

Carausius said 'To my death? Maximian has no mercy.'

Quintus stands alone, dressed in useless finery. Humiliated in front of the troops, abandoned by his escort he can only turn and walk angrily away. As he leaves, the port echoes to cries of 'Hail Carausius' and these reverberate around his head for the crossing. Worse than that was the laughter that followed him.

He orders the captain of the transport to leave immediately. Seeing the expression on his face, the captain dare not argue, and they sail into the darkness and the peril of a night crossing with a tired crew. He wonders what on earth he can say to Maximian that won't make his position worse. We have triggered a bigger problem than pirates, he muses. At Boulogne he has to find himself a horse, which makes him feel belittled as his uniform betrays his senior rank. By the time he reached the palace a week has passed, but he is aware that he must break the news as nothing could have got there quicker unless travelling by day and night.

At his palace, Maximian, Constantius and several advisers are there to witness Quintus's embarrassment. Probably better than facing him alone, he thinks, and wishes he was anywhere else. I'd rather face a whole tribe of angry barbarians on my own.

'Well, where is he?' demanded Maximian, getting more red-faced at the obvious discomfort of his representative.

'I told him of his arrest, but he refused me.' he said.

'I didn't expect him to come quietly, did you?' said Maximian quietly, giving Quintus a glare through which his growing anger shone through.

'What about your escort? They had the power to drag him if necessary. Or you could have done as I suggested and killed him there and then.'

Quintus replied 'They refused me too. They refused my orders. No-one in the port from Marcellus downwards lifted a finger to help me. I had no option but to leave and cross back to Gaul. You will not want to hear this, but he seems to have the support and loyalty of everyone there. They were shouting 'Hail Carausius' the way they did after the battle. He seems to mesmerise people for some reason and they want to follow him. I think we have the danger of a new emperor to fight.'

Saying it this way I was declaring my loyalty to Maximian while expressing my fears.

Constantius interjected 'I think we need to seek intelligence about this disaster. Quintus, I think your influence in Britain has just ended.'

Maximian replied 'Yes, send out messengers in disguise if necessary, and find out what in Hades is going on. Quintus, you will stay here.'

I felt as if I had been put under arrest myself, although it was implied rather than stated. For the first time among these men, I felt unsafe and untrusted.

Over the next few weeks the news got steadily worse. Carausius had indeed declared himself emperor of Britain, the legions there had declared their support, and he had just received the news that two legions in Gaul also rebelled in his favour. He not only held possession of the entire Roman navy of Britain but also the port of Boulogne. Some of the Frankish tribes to the south that were never really accepting of Roman rule had also voiced their support. Furthermore, income from the lands had stopped and the supply of food and other materials was likely to run out. Aware of their importance, Maximian was irate.

'This is an insult to me and the empire. I will drag him to Rome itself in chains and have him publicly executed. Unlike Caratacus, no fine speeches will save him from my anger.'

Chapter 17

Carausius

Carausius stands on the jetty, stunned by what has happened. From the success of his campaign against the pirates he was not expecting such a turnaround in his fortunes. He knew he was an outsider and others would leech off his success, but some thanks and his freedom to return home would have sufficed. With cheers and shouts of support ringing in his ears, he realised, that like Julius Caesar before, he had crossed a Rubicon. He could not imagine any forgiveness in Maximian, or even the chance of a fair hearing. He had felt, and others had warned him that Maximian held a jealousy against him for his ability to lead and command the loyalty of his men. Quite how he did this he was not sure himself. It was true that he led from the front and did not expect anything of anyone that he would not do himself, but that's what all leaders should do, he thought. Interrupting his thoughts, Allectus pushes through the throng of people and put an arm around his shoulder.

'I can't quite believe this. You have done what Maximian bid of you, with more success than I think even he thought likely. There's no going back now. Quintus will be a vengeful enemy after being humiliated like that. Even his own men deserted him and have sided with you. He is on his way to report to Maximian and we know what he will say. He was tied up with this venture too so he will tell of your treachery and disloyalty to save himself.'

Carausius looks at him. 'Do you think Maximian saw me as a competitor? I never wanted to be an emperor, it never crossed my mind. I would rather be home in Wales with my family and live the life for which I was intended.'

'Well, putting yourself in his shoes, he wants and needs absolute power. His reputation will be of a strong ruler who expanded the empire. Without that he is in danger from other ambitious men. Consider how short the rules of some emperors were. You have qualities which he does not and that brings out the ability of your men to give of themselves and perform well, give their very best as they believe in you.' He laughs 'You certainly have destroyed that for him. His only chance is to destroy us completely.'

Carausius replies 'Thank you my cousin, I realise I have brought you to this.'

'Not just me' Allectus says wryly, 'I think everyone who supports you realises that they are putting their lives on the line for you.'

Later, Carausius and Allectus are dining in the great fortress with Marcellus and Tertius. The mood is sombre as the situation sinks home.

'If I declare myself emperor of Britain, how in Hades do I run an empire?'

The mood strangely lifts.

Allectus says 'We can work this out. You need a team of advisers who are close to you,' he beams at Marcellus and Tertius 'and you need to establish relationships with the tribal rulers of the island. Remember I have seen the workings of this part of the empire. Ruling is not easy, sometimes tough and unpopular decisions have to be made. It's a fact that for the poorest people, if they are treated fairly, who is in charge matters less than the quality of their lives.'

Marcellus interjects 'I know the navy and I can go back to commanding the port, and Tertius here...'

Tertius booms 'I know the army like the back of my hand.'

Carausius says 'You are making this sound easy, you have my greatest thanks....'

Allectus continues 'The tribal leaders will need more careful handling. They have pride in their cultures and do not all like to be under what they will still see as imperial rule. Think of my father, for heaven's sake,' he laughs, 'and compare him with your's as someone who can compromise and flourish as a result.'

Carausius says 'You are making much sense, and I can now see a strategy forming. Maximian will not hear for a few days yet and there is little he can do for a while as I have his ships.'

They nod and laugh at this, and the atmosphere becomes visibly relaxed.

'Let's enjoy this fine meal and drink the emperor's fine wines. We will meet tomorrow when we are fresh.'

Establishing the team with Allectus, Marcellus and Tertius was popular with the troops who knew them well by now. There was an overall mood of uncertainty, and wondering what, if and when something would happen. They knew of Maximian, either having met and fought for him, or by reputation. Neither diminished the feeling that there would eventually be an assault on Britain. Carausius was happy to delegate the military roles to his new commanders, and appointed Allectus as his Minister of Finance. The latter had pointed out that everything eventually came down to money; the maintenance of the military strength they had, plus the need for expansion of defences against the eventual invasion, whenever it might be. While Carausius was planning his taking over an imperial role, he smiled to himself that he would need to follow in the footsteps of the first visits following the appointment of Quintus. Thinking of him, he realised that as emperor he should make his base in London. He knew that there was a governor's palace and thought that he could bring Anwen, Alys and the new child that he had not met to live with him. He wondered how he would explain to Anwen how he was now Emperor of Britain.

Reports kept coming in of growing support for his rule. What he could not understand was why this was.

'I know I have a good reputation with the army and,

since the pirate business, the navy, but people who do not know me are rising in my name.'

Allectus looked him in the eye, and said 'I think it is more than just you. People have been growing unhappy with Maximian's rule. They know he is brutal, ambitious and feared rather than respected. He has never visited Britain yet people are taxed to serve his purposes. They do not like being ruled by a total stranger from so far away whose only interest in them is to take a share of what they own and earn. You are seen as brave and honourable and supportive of people while being one of them. You represent changing times and have become the man of the moment.'

Tertius added 'The soldiers here feel abandoned. Most are far from home and their agreement with Rome is for regular pay and the promise of citizenship and lands when they have served their time. Records seem poor and incorrect, so they see no clear future, and beyond that, they are bored and that makes morale and discipline harder to support or impose.'

As organisational structures were being established and officials appointed, there was surprising and pleasing news as well from northern Gaul. Two complete legions under Decimus's control had rebelled against Maximian in his support. Several Frankish tribal groups also declared loyalty. Not only did he have more soldiers he could call on, but equally importantly the naval and military port of Boulogne, with this southern section of the Roman navy. With this military force, he realised that he had naval supremacy that was complete and absolute. He now controlled the great channel on both sides.

Unless there was a major change in fortune, Maximian was now powerless to launch an invasion.

Before his move to London, he gathered Darius and the men and took a quick trip across the channel to Boulogne to visit Decimus and inform of his plans. Helming his ship gave him an opportunity to enjoy his relationship with the sea. They greeted each other as old friends and the support of the soldiers for their leader and their new emperor was evident. He formally appointed him as commander of the Gaulish legions and emphasised the obvious task of securing these southern borders.

He travelled to London with Allectus and as that young man had so many years ago he marvelled at the fine stone buildings and the layout of the city. Even his enthusiastic descriptions could not describe the reality. The great stone walls were lined with city folk and soldiers, most cheering with cries of 'Hail Carausius' from the soldiers, and clapping and yelling from the civilians. The news had spread ahead of him and it seemed as if the city was waiting for him. As they progressed towards the centre, they headed for the governor's house which had been suggested to be reclaimed as the emperor's palace.

When they reached it, he hesitated on the doorstep and said to Allectus 'This is unreal.'

Allectus laughed and said 'You had better get used to this. Tomorrow I will instruct you in politics and have your tailor make you some togas - having usurped the purple you now have to show it to the people.'

Carausius walked around his palace and admired the frescoes, the mosaics and found the bathroom, with a large sunken bathtub decorated with the finest tiles. There were resident staff with a housekeeper in charge and some slaves who were unclear about what had happened and what might be the consequence. He took time to introduce himself and explain. They realised that he was a decent man who had a distant family with which he was longing to be reconciled, and he saw how his family would be accommodated and cared for. Even the prospect of young children seemed to bring out a welcome. In the great offices, he saw how at ease Allectus was with the people. He was introduced to the administrators, the back room men who set taxes and ensured that accounts were recorded. Just like the peasants, he thought, if they are treated well and with respect from me we will all get on fine.

Anwen, Alys and his new daughter who had been called Bronwen, named after a daughter of a very old sea god, arrived to a chorus of shrieks and giggles as they dismounted from their carriage. As a girl from a small town so far away, she couldn't quite believe that she was now an empress, and collapsed in laughter when Carausius called her that. As they settled in, the housekeeper saw that Anwen seemed lost in her new circumstances and breaking with protocol ignored that she was the emperor's wife and took her under her wing. She told her how the palace was run and where she might find clothing and other things she needed. Alys was now eight years old, and had grown into a confident curious little girl. She enchanted the staff and if she couldn't get people to chase her would continue in dogged pursuit of them. Bronwen was four and to his sadness Carausius realised that he had missed her childhood. She was dark-haired and more serious in nature, but still chased and followed her bigger sister around the palace. In his message to Anwen he had warned her of what to expect in London, and he enjoyed the wide-eyed way in which she gazed at the sights. She soon determined to make the palace more homely, with fabrics she found in the local markets. Bath times for the children became very wet affairs and such was the size of it that Anwen was teaching them to swim. Once they were settled in and restored to their lives together, it was time for Carausius to explore his new empire. After he had left, there were times when she felt lost in a very different world from her roots. She wondered when she would see her parents again, and knew they would not travel all the way to London. Still, she thought, we must make the best of it, and the children were thriving here. She did worry that her wonderful but impulsive husband would run into problems he could not control.

Carausius had maintained the group of soldiers that had formed Quintus's escort guard, and to reward them for their loyalty to him promoted them to his imperial guard. He recruited another group to increase the security of their mission, with outriders and scouts to forge ahead to seek out threats. With Allectus and a team from his treasury to keep records, they first went north. Carausius was aware that too much projection of power was not always welcomed, and with as much intelligence about the individual tribes he could glean, set the numbers of his troops and his style of dress accordingly. They followed the lines of many of the roads that the Romans had built and travelled from fort to fort, eventually reaching the great Roman city of York. North of this the lands became hostile. He walked along the great wall of emperor Hadrian and spoke with the soldiers who manned the forts that studded the length of it. Standing on the top, he thought he saw a group of painted warriors in the misty distance, but a swirl of moisture obscured his view. When it had moved he could see nothing.

They travelled west then south and finally went to the extremes of their parents' lands. His father greeted him with amusement and he found it impossible to maintain and project his dignity. His older brothers could only tease him, and while there was concern for his overall situation, it was only his mother who showed it. He and Allectus were astonished to see the change in Arthfael. His developing prosperity had wrought many changes. His house had been rebuilt in stone and his clothes were fresh and clean.

'Quite the businessman, father' said Allectus. 'You will be a Roman yet!'

'Huh, the day you get me in a toga will be when I am laid in my coffin, son. I must admit though, I have found some benefits of playing along.'

Carausius called on Anwen's parents to reassure them and described their new life together. They were still bemused at the astonishing change of circumstances.

They duly returned to London and held a council

meeting to take stock. Carausius reports first that he felt that there were no problems with the tribal relationships.

'Some are friendlier than others, and I can see that the Romans have influenced and included some younger men and children in the way that we were taken. I can see good and bad in that, but I would have to say more good. Mind you, without that we would be growing old in our lands in the ways of generations before. We have to accept that the world changes.'

Allectus and his team reported on the financial side of taxes and tributes. 'As these payments are longstanding and unchanged, they are accepted. My worry is when things have to change,' he says, 'you are concerned about getting on with people, but we have to counter that with the expenses we have talked about. There have been problems for years with the coinage being debased. Less silver and gold are being put into smaller coins, from the mints in Britain and Gaul. These buy less as prices rise, and confidence in the system falls. We need to think about this as we have decided to extend and fortify the forts along the shores of south-eastern and southern Britain. They will need garrisons and they need feeding and arming. Marcellus wants more faster small warships in anticipation of defeating the invasion when it comes. We have to be prepared and ready now before such a thing gets close. I calculate it may be several years before Maximian can build a fleet, and I can estimate the likely costs and see that it will pose the same problems for him, possibly worse as he has lost the income from Britain.'

'What can we do?' asks Carausius.

Allectus takes out a purse and scatters coins onto the table. 'What do you see?'

Carausius raises and eyebrow quizzically.

'No, what do you see?'

'Well, money, obviously,' he replies.

Allectus says, 'It is more than that. Maybe for most people they see value and what they can buy, but look at the claims and boasts written on them. They carry a message. Those who can't read see your face and your strength; those who can see more. Look at how Maximian likens himself to Hercules and Diocletian to Jove. These are powerful messages.

'I see that', says Carausius, 'but what shall we do?'

'We will first order our mints to produce our own coinage. These will have your name, status and silhouette on them and it will be very clear that this money is ours. Our coins will carry messages of peace, security and show you as a restorer of Britain,' replies Allectus. 'You should declare you imperial status by adopting a full Roman name. Marcus Aurelius Carausius Augustus or something similar. After that we will have to look at how we administer our new lands, and what and how much we need to tax.'

Chapter 18

Maximian

Angered almost beyond his own comprehension, Maximian now started issuing orders for the construction of an invasion fleet of transports and barges. Up-river shipyards along the coast clear of attack from Britain were seized to build a fleet of transports. He declared that he wants to move two legions into Britain. He appointed men in charge to make sure his demands are carried out and summoned them to his palace. He gathered them together and harangued them. Threatened with severe consequence for failure, and followed by 'If at first you don't succeed, your successors surely will,' they left for the coast in a worried mood. They recognised that they would be in competition for wood, nails and skilled workmen and that triggered a rush to get organised. Inevitably there were delay, bottlenecks and because of the haste, more injuries among the ship-workers. Despite the threats and bluster of Maximian, it took the best part of two years for the complete fleet to be constructed.

While this fleet was finally assembled and loaded with arms and soldiers, travellers and fishermen made reports of sightings of it to Dover. Marcellus sent messengers to Carausius who returned to take charge. Ships were prepared for battle, crews trained and rehearsed, and reconnaissance voyages made by the nighthawks. As the invasion fleet was sighted, Carausius released his warships. The day that Maximian's fleet sailed was confused and overcast. The ships were initially gathered together and the sea was choppy. Packed in together, many sailors became sea-sick, and as the ships were rowed into the great channel, the wind started increasing. The pull of the tides were strong as the moon was at its greatest, and slowly the great fleet started to spread. The waiting warships of Carausius watched from the distance as the rowers became exhausted, and their rhythm became uncoordinated. The high sided transports lurched and rolled; some started taking in water. The few that got further into the channel were attacked and boarded by the savage and battle-hardened troops of Tertius. Bodies were thrown into the sea. Those that could float drifted slowly back to land. The lower-hulled barges were swamped by the larger waves further from the shore and slowly panic spread and those ships that could returned to the land. After all the work and preparation, it was clear that the invasion had failed. Carausius now ruled supreme and secure on the island of Britain.

'What the hell happened?' demanded Maximian, 'Tell me what happened exactly.'

The tale was told and the costs in lives and money measured. Constantius, now appointed his deputy as Praetorian Prefect, gave the detail. His narrow face took on a neutral expression as he outlined the facts.

'The fleet gathered as planned with our soldiers on board. The weather changed for the worse and the ships couldn't deal with the wind and waves. They were designed for a straight journey across on a calm sea. The captains assured me that they knew the tides, but they were strong and carried some of the ships away. The rowers could not hold them and became fatigued. Some barges foundered and we lost many soldiers. Even if they could swim their armour carried them down.'

Maximian asked coldly 'And what of Carausius and his fleet?'

'His ships were alerted but few went into action. They were ready, though, and if we had progressed further we would have seen even more losses.'

Maximian started to rant. 'This is a disaster for us, for me. That renegade is now sunning himself with thoughts of a victory he didn't deserve.'

Constantius replied as tactfully as he could 'What's done is done. We must learn and bide our time, your imperial majesty. We will take our revenge in due time and savour it. In the meantime...' he hesitated, 'Perhaps a word with Diocletian He is still your senior and it is better he hears from you rather than by rumour.'

Maximian thinks for a moment. Calming himself down, he said 'You offer wise counsel, I will follow it although I am uncomfortable about declaring a failure; it is not something I have had to do before.'

Maximian travelled to meet Diocletian who is campaigning and meet at Carnuntum near the great river Danube. After seizing the empire, Diocletian had realised that it was just too big to be ruled effectively by one man. There were too many potential threats, within and without its borders, and the travelling time for messages and other intelligence was too slow. He divided the whole empire into four parts and appointed three others to rule as a 'tetrarchy'. This vision, and his management skills had made this system function well at this time.

At an audience with the emperor who appointed him he calmly explains the reality of the situation.

Diocletian looked thoughtful and said 'You have appeared to have created a monster and we are now in a situation where we cannot do anything to change that for now. In the long term we must reclaim Britain, but for now we need some of the things we got from it. Tell me, what sort of a man Carausius is, and what diplomacy can we call on?'

Relaxing on a couch with a cup of wine and with the man who was his mentor, Maximian was able to put aside his emotions for once.

'He is an interesting man. He was taken by my envoy Quintus as a hostage and put into our military. He is a son of a family of seafarers and traders who settled in Wales a few hundred years ago. From the start he showed intelligence and initiative and has an uncanny ability to gain mens' respect and loyalty. He led some of my troops and turned a defeat into a victory. As I result I allowed his return to his family in the extreme west of Wales. However, perhaps unfortunately, he saved Quintus's life when he took over command of our ship in a great storm on his journey to his homelands. As a result, when I had no experienced captains or suitable ships to tackle the pirate raids, Quintus raised his name. The rest you know. I don't know if he kept money for himself as claimed. Too many people would start rumours through jealousy, I fear.'

'Did you want to believe it?' asked Diocletian.

Maximian hesitated. 'I did dislike what he had become, I think.'

Passing over this and knowing the reasons behind it, Diocletian said 'Let's think about what we need. Revenge will come later. What has happened to our trade? Gold, iron, grain, we used to get and are now seeing shortages.'

Maximian replied 'Not much moves, really. We couldn't collect goods because Carausius controls the channel.'

Diocletian said thoughtfully 'We still have Quintus as a go-between. He needs to redeem himself and that gives us a hold over him. Send him under a flag of truce. Tell him we wish to restore trade and give him authority to agree fair prices. If he establishes a good relationship he may mention that if he surrenders and returns Britain we will treat him leniently. I know you want revenge but this is about more than your pride. The more this gets around the empire the more trouble and instability could arise. But whatever, we need to make an agreement here.'

Maximian thought and said 'If he won't surrender, what can we do?'

Diocletian replied 'Let's be realistic here. He has an island, he has our navy, and we do not, he controls the seas and we want to trade. I realise that he will use money to strengthen his defences, who wouldn't, but my dear friend, look at this. You won't like this but as a last resort, we should tell him that we accept the situation, we recognise his abilities and strengths and that we accept he can rule Britain as an emperor with our approval.'

At this, Maximian looked appalled. 'You cannot mean this. He has humiliated all of us with this rebellion. I want him dead.'

'As I implied, we must bide our time. We have no means to invade and when we do we must have a large force and not fail this time. Quintus can look out for tensions and difficulties within his administration. It is hard for a man who is not ruthless to rule, and I suspect that our man cares too much for his followers – I call them that because of how you describe his nature. That could be his downfall.'

Maximian took his leave and travelled back to where Quintus, having been ordered to attend, was waiting anxiously. On the journey he mulled over what was said and came to realised that there was no alternative, for now, he told himself.

He summoned Quintus and said 'You have some responsibility for this mess and you are going to help us get out of it.'

He explained that he was appointing him as ambassador to the court of Carausius.

'You will negotiate to get our trade going, and as you know this man and have some mutual respect, you will also pass on a message from Diocletian and me that if he will surrenders we will treat him well. Try to get him to believe that.'

Quintus looked sceptical.

'I know,' Maximian continued 'but if that fails then we will have to accept the reality of the situation and accept that he does rule Britain and we can do nothing about it. You may tell him then that we will accept that and allow his position as emperor of Britain. Those are Diocletian's words; I would choke on them if I had to say them .'

Quintus looked astonished. 'I can't believe that you would agree to do that. It makes his position legitimate and even stronger.'

Maximian said 'I know, but he may start making mistakes that will weaken him. Believe me, when things settle down, I will still be planning my invasion. I will get my revenge.'

Constantius, listening carefully, shrugged and said 'Sensible advice, I suppose' and made sure that he was seen as detached from the decision.

Chapter 19

Quintus

Another impossible task from this impossible man, he thought. The thought of returning to the country of his humiliation was almost too much. I am a military man. I am trained to kill, not talk. I will have to face this man for whom I am held responsible. Since our lives became entwined I have not escaped being linked with his fate. Taking two soldiers as escorts to give him some semblance of authority, they rode for the coast. He had to travel north to find a port away from Carausius's control that had a ship to take them. Once again he had to suffer the crossing of the great channel that this time was even longer. He decided that he hated ships and anything to do with them and looked anxiously at the horizon for approaching bad weather. Not much troubled him, but memories of the storm do return to him from time to time in dreams in the dark nights. They entered the harbour at Dover under a white flag of truce and he walked quickly past the jetty that held the memory of his humiliation. He was regarded curiously by some of the soldiers. Some ignored him while a couple almost saluted, to his bitter amusement. Taking horses, they headed for London. Little seemed to have changed in the feel of the countryside and as they entered through the great walls of London, Quintus felt a yearning for the times before this present disaster. He arranged for his soldiers and horses to be settled into a barrack block. It was strange for him to explain his position, and as a former senior officer he loathed the feeling that he was a supplicant. He was, however, greeted in good grace and not made to feel unwelcome. For a moment he wondered about the loyalty of his escort. Might they be likely to defect as well? As he approached his old palace, Carausius emerged carrying his younger daughter. News of his arrival preceded him, he thought.

Quintus felt a pang of regret for his austere military life, but gathered himself and said accusingly 'You are living in my house!' Recovering himself, he added 'Greetings Carausius, I am here as ambassador from Maximian'.

Carausius said 'You are welcome too. Come and take some refreshment. With children around you will find it less tidy.'

They settled down in an informal manner, and Quintus started to follow his brief. 'You know Maximian will not let up. He will build another invasion fleet, and another if necessary until he had defeated you. You will learn the responsibilities of power, and they are hard. You and I have both fought battles and we know when we have lost. I believe Maximian could be persuaded to treat you leniently if you were return these lands to Rome.'

Carausius responded angrily 'I don't believe that for a minute. I have seen how he treats prisoners and those he has conquered. Your historian Tacitus quoted an enemy of Rome who said you create a desert and call it peace. That is Maximian and what he does. Look how he ordered my arrest and execution. No chance of a trial, no evidence, as I kept nothing for myself and just the word of a someone with a reason to undermine me. It wasn't you, was it?'

'No, of course not' responded Quintus 'we may be on opposite sides but I respect you and will not forget that you saved my life. I just don't understand you. After all, you are almost a Roman.'

Ignoring what he might have taken as a slight rather than the confused compliment that was meant, Carausius continued 'and as for attacking pirate ships after they had raided, that was just sensible strategy. They sail slower, the crews are tired and the night is dark but passing when they return to their lands. I would lose more men by attacking when they are alert and fired up at the thought of plunder or women.'

Quintus said 'But you are a sailor, a prince of your lands, wouldn't you like to return to all that?'

'There is nothing I would like more but the fates have dealt me this hand and I must play my best' replied Carausius.

Quintus warned 'There is so much which is unfamiliar to you, you have no time to learn.'

Carausius said 'Let me remind you of the support I have from the army, the navy and the people. The systems you had in place are still there and I believe the people are ready to continue. Anyway you forget about my cousin. He knows about these things. You and I, we read battles, he reads balance sheets; we read lines of men and he reads lines of figures. Do you know what is ironic?' he asked quizzically.

'No' said Quintus warily.

'Allectus is much a creation of yours as I am. You took him from the muddy streets of Siluria and his overwhelming father and sent him here. You perhaps accidently put him where he could flourish. Like you I first saw him as weak and perhaps overlooked him. He didn't join in games with my brothers and me. I think he didn't want to lose, and knew he would. I brought him along because he was lost where he was. Now he has a talent superior to most. You had a good insight into our potentials but could not predict where these would lead.'

Quintus replied 'By all the gods, if Maximian realises this I am doubly doomed, I would never have any chance of forgiveness.'

Carausius concluded the conversation. 'Tomorrow you will address my council as Maximian's ambassador and we will hear what you want to tell us. But remember there is to be no talk of surrender. That is not in question, Britain is mine.'

Quintus turned to leave, almost spoke but hesitated and waved a casual salute. He has decided to save the final part of his instructions until the meeting.

The next morning, he left his lodging house and walked through the familiar streets to the council chamber. This truly is a fine city, he thought, and remembered the respect that his position as Maximian's envoy gained him. Now he has to negotiate, nor give orders. Recognising the reality of the whole situation he determined to go straight to the point.

Arriving at the building he was asked to wait in an anteroom until he was called. Summoned like a servant, he thought.

The council was comprised of Allectus and Valentinus from the treasury, a pair of dignitaries from the city administration and Titus representing the armed forces. Two of the nearest tribal leaders were also present as Carausius thought it a tactful way of communicating his intentions. A scribe was in attendance to keep a record.

After pleasantries and having dealt with some unfinished business, Carausius addressed the meeting.

'Our old friend Quintus, who most of you will remember from his position as official envoy, is now here as ambassador from the court of Maximian. He wishes to address us and we need to hear what he is going to say.'

Quintus was called in and came straight to his point. 'I don't go with this diplomatic flim-flam so let me say that I am authorised by their imperial highnesses, emperors Diocletian of the eastern Roman empire and Maximian, of the western Roman empire, to say to you, Carausius, that your position as emperor of Britain is formally recognised, by both of them.'

At this pronouncement there was a stunned silence.

'Wiser counsels have prevailed, and with this we can talk about our future relationships', he continued. 'you know me, I am a simple soldier, a military man. I do not have the smooth tongue of a diplomat so may I get to the heart of all this?' After nods all round, he said 'Outside the military situation there is the issue of trade. Rome has always purchased, at fair prices, goods such as grains, wool, mineral, gold and in return you through your traders have imported wines, oils, and, you know, other things you want. I propose that we restore these activities to our mutual benefit. With your agreement, I will bring over a delegation to set up and negotiate these matters. I will await your reply.' He added wholeheartedly 'If you agree, I can return to my homelands and leave this behind.'

He stood up, saluted, turned and walked out. As the door closed behind him, there was a collective exhalation of breath. The tribal leaders appeared unmoved, but Allectus said 'That is the last thing I expected to hear. I was expecting to be harangued about surrender and threatened with all sorts of retribution.'

Carausius said 'He came to see me yesterday and I disabused him of any idea of surrender. He did recognise that we did, or to be fair mostly you, have the wherewithal to run an empire. The other emperors know the situation too, but he kept their acceptance well up his sleeve, I must say.'

Tertius interjected 'I'm not sure that we should see ourselves as safe. I wouldn't trust any of them as far as...'

'I know', replied Carausius, 'We must always keep up our guard. It's the weak who attract attack, history always tells us.'

Allectus said 'Let's talk further about this. We need to think of formal agreements, prices, transport costs...'

Carausius, seeing that Allectus was in full flow, interrupted 'Valentinus, can we find a space for this delegation in the treasury. While I don't want them to see our state secrets, it must be beneficial to have them close at hand.'

Valentinus nodded in agreement, so Carausius said 'I will let Quintus know our decisions.'

Chapter 20

Allectus

I was enjoying my job as minister of finance. I liked the title, the task and have confidence in myself. I have found a house that suits my needs and employed a pair of servants to clean and cook. I remember how I visited my old workplace at the treasury for the first time. It was a fine dry day, the sun was shining and the city was bustling with activity. Dressed in my finest, I mounted the steps to the great bronze-clad doors. I gave them a push and so well-oiled were they that they crashed open, with such force that everything stopped. Aware of my accidentally impressive entrance I looked around as my eyes adjusted from the bright sunlight outside. Inside was much as I remembered it. There was Valentinus, with his scribes and clerks surrounded by papers and documents, and it took a moment for him to recognise me. Ever the professional financier, he sounded wary.

'Allectus, I had heard of your elevation. You have come a long way from that shy lad we took in. I must say you look the part now. I suppose you are now my master, and that of all of us. We have been running this part of the empire for years and there may be some divided loyalties, I am sure, but I know that Carausius is accepted by the people, and most importantly of course the army. We must discuss how we proceed, assuming that's what you want. Maximian has always been a distant figure and we live comfortably enough here, as you know, well away from him. He has never even visited this island, which may be just as well knowing his reputation.

Quintus is, or was, his man but despite being a bit, how shall I say, rough around the edges, he was more than happy to leave us to it. I like to think from respect, but possibly he realised that what we do is beyond him.'

Allectus replied 'I agree with what you say. A change at the top does not mean everything should be torn up to start again. In many ways, what you perceive in Quintus is present in my cousin. That does not make him a bad man, indeed as a member of my family I have a love for him. But we have different skills. If we have a battle, you would trust Carausius to lead and we would follow without question. Together we will succeed.'

We sat down, took refreshment and I was amused at the slower and more calculated pace of life in an office. We discussed the need to maintain our income and financial flows, and how there would be a call on the expenditure to bolster our defences. Valentinus nodded, and our discussions turned to trade and the implications of the political situation. In a way, I felt that I had come home.

Leaving the treasury, I had one more task before I returned to my house. Walking along an old familiar route I arrived at the home of Valentinus and his family, where I had lived for my four years in London. I knocked on the door and was admitted to the grand reception room where I was joined by Livia. She was surprised to see me, and greeted me kindly. We discussed the politics to get this out of the way. I was able to reassure her that nothing much would change although we feared the wrath of Maximian. I added that we had made him impotent by seizing the entire channel fleet.

She gave a wry smile, then 'I am forgetting my manners. You will take refreshment with me?'

I said 'Of course, that would be good. I am thirsty after a long meeting I held with Valentinus and his team at the treasury.'

She looked at me directly 'May I ask you, will there be changes?'

I looked her. I saw a concern in her eyes and recognising this and the reason, I replied 'I am in charge as minister of finance in this government. I know how well Valentinus runs the department. I learned from him, after all. I think little needs to change as far as the people there. I know there was concern that we would just throw people out, but there is still a state to run and no-one better than him to do it.'

She looked relieved and I added 'The people welcomed the change when Carausius declared himself emperor. We were both surprised at the support, to be honest. Carausius was to be executed, on false charges, I may say, and I was linked to him so our fates were mixed up. Respect and admiration for him and a dislike of Maximian and his methods carried the day.'

A door opened and Chresima came in carrying a tray of drinks and biscuits. I felt as if I was hit by a thunderbolt. She was as elegant as ever, her hair up in the braided way she wore it, and in the simple white shift that she carried so well. I could not look away, I just could not. I noted the sweetness in her face and that she had gained a few little lines around her mouth. I thought they added to her charm. She looked back at me, calmly.

'If I may speak, mistress, it's good to see you, Allectus.'

'You too,' I replied, almost stumbling in my speech.

My mouth was dry and my heart was beating faster than I think ever before. I became aware that Livia was saying something, but she stopped when she realised that my eyes were elsewhere.

'Put that tray down, girl.' she ordered Chresima, who gathered herself to do that. At this I realised that she had been looking back at me too. Livia told her firmly 'Pour the drinks, Allectus is thirsty.'

She muttered to me 'And not just for a drink I see. Don't think I don't know what went on in this house.'

Chresima hovered, her pose asking if she should leave and her face looking slightly pink. Mine must have been as purple as the stripe on Carausius's toga. Livia looked at her, with a curious expression on her face.

'You may stay a while. I have to check something in the kitchens and we must not abandon our guest.'

We were left together, I a minister of finance and she a slave girl.

'I've thought of you often' I said.

She replied 'I have heard things from the family and know you are part of the rebellion. Are you in danger?'

'No', I said, 'We are popular and on an island.'

I sat her down and explained the situation to her. She gradually relaxed and started to talk about her life. While she did, our eyes barely left each other, and I knew I would have to address what was unsaid.

Livia returned, opening the door slowly. I wished that Chresima and I had kissed. Livia started bustling about loading the tray and before I could say anything, she started saying how empty and quiet the house was now that Marcus was now away serving as a junior diplomat in Rome itself.

I thought that she was just telling me how proud she was of his progress until she said 'We don't really need all these staff in this house. I don't know what to do, perhaps you could advise me?'

Having recovered some of my composure, I said 'It must be hard getting rid of people you have known a long time, especially if they are hard-working and loyal.'

And so it was that Chresima came to live with me.

Chapter 21

Carausius

The country seemed mostly quiet. I got reports of periodic disturbances in various places and was happy in principle for the tribal leaders to deal with them; after all these things were usually against their interests as well but I became aware of two problems. The first was that the Roman policy against holding significant amounts of arms prevented this, and the other was that there was an expectation that I would sort out even the minor matters. I summoned Tertius to talk about this. He warned me of the consequences of letting the tribes arm. He has had experience of squabbles turning into major fights. Although the tribal barriers seem defined, there were always desires for more land or to sort out differences with violence. I discussed this at my council meetings but we failed to come up with a clear solution. It all depended on where the tribe lived, how serious the matter was, and how war-like and willing to resort to violence the particular tribe was.

As we had not interfered with the military structures, I assumed that there was the network of forts around the major roads that we, or rather the Romans (because I can't really think of myself as one) had constructed for rapid mobility. These extended as far north as the great wall and as far west as my own lands. I have three legions of troops in Britain and the two commanded by Decimus in Gaul. I asked Tertius for suggestions. He was close to his men and I could rely on him for pragmatic advice with the honesty that comes from not being afraid to disagree. What he said, though, started to worry me.

'Remember, many of these men are far from home. They signed up with the promise that after their term of service they would be given lands and could retire with honour. We now have lost those links. Even getting messages from their homes is hindered. What is worse is that, as Allectus will tell you, the price of goods has been rising and their wages have not. Boredom patrolling peaceful lands on top, I am concerned their loyalty could weaken. Some units have grown soft and may need a firmer hand in charge.'

Hearing this lowered my spirits. My reputation could only carry so far, and they held expectations of me that might become difficult to fulfill. I confided in Tertius.

'This is important. Our safety depends on this and if the leaders expect our protection they should be assured that they can get it. I know we can move forces about quickly with the roads, and some unoccupied forts can be made ready again.'

This was the strength of a Roman army, after all, based on discipline morale and a sense of purpose. I realised I was coming up with my solution.

'Tertius, I want an inventory of all our troops. I want to know where they are from, how old they are and how long they have been serving. I want a breakdown of wages from rank to rank, and ask Allectus for the overall costs in wages and support.'

I knew we needed to build morale and restore a sense of pride in their roles. I knew part of this meant showing myself and that I would have to travel around the country again. Tertius sent messengers to all units. I think once I have the results of this census, I can release those men whose terms are nearly up. Their ability to fight may be limited through age and once paid off, we can recruit more. After all, many of the soldiers were local Britons seeking a good career and I know marriages between the other soldiers and local women occur. Those who have put down roots here may well want to settle down here. I met again with Tertius, informed him of my plans and ordered him to assemble a platoon of troops with horses to accompany us when we were ready.

There was no disagreement in council, although I was warned that I would have to deliver on any promises I made. Allectus expressed concern about the budget after I had said that I may need to purchase land from the tribes for any settlers. We were producing coins at our mints, even the one at Rouen in Gaul, so that did not seem to be a problem for me.

I took my leave of my family and we set off. Romans have usually built their forts to similar designs; even the great legionary bases are laid out to the same plan, so I quickly became accustomed to them and could concentrate on the soldiers. I met many young officers who impressed me and a few who did not. Some were promoted and others brought down in the ranks and for fairness to be seen, all decisions were explained. Tertius and I made speeches of encouragement and set new rates of pay for all ranks. I checked on supply lines and encouraged the use of the local tribes for food that could be supplied locally. Having seen it work bilaterally, I knew that bolstering the local economy would be beneficial. Warning of our coming brought out the best in the officers, who saw to it that armour was polished and repaired to fortifications were made. Overall I was happy with what I saw and hoped that the way we had gone about this achieved what I wanted.

We were just heading south when we received unwelcome news. A large band of Pictish warriors from Caledonia had broken through the great wall of Emperor Hadrian, overwhelming the local garrison. There had been many deaths and this band was now ravaging and looting the countryside. We turned around, headed back north and sought information to assist us. Small raids were common and usually limited, but this was of a greater scale. The Pictish leader was called Domnall and had a brutish reputation. His warriors daubed themselves in the blue dyes for which they were famous and through alcohol or strange potions were made fearless. They were said to mutilate their skin with paints and needles. The estimate of his strength that I am given was of more than a thousand men. There was a battle ahead that I must win because there was more at stake than just land and pillaging; my position as emperor and its acceptance by the people was under challenge. I knew that I must act and I must not fail.

Retracing our footsteps, we gathered troops from the forts we now passed. I sent messengers to the forts further along the wall to assemble another army to approach from the north. While I was looked to as leader, I consulted with the officers about the terrain where we might have to fight. I did not know these lands and would prefer to fight on ground of my own choosing. With Tertius close at hand, we drew maps of hills, rivers and any other obstacles that could influence the battle. I also warned of the danger of how I knew that some barbarians carried long axes and how they could be used against us, recounting my experience in Gaul. After two days of fast marching, our scouts told us that the Picts had been sighted. Smoke was rising in the distance and peasants were seen fleeing towards us. We made camp, posted sentries and tried to rest. I wanted my men fresh for the next day.

Before dawn broke, Tertius and I rode out in an easterly direction for a couple of miles. I had no doubt that the Picts had scouts looking for any resistance and on finding an army's worth would be keeping us under observation. The ground was undulating with small valleys and ridges so we were able to keep ourselves from the skyline as we now turned north. When we were close, we tied the horses to a tree and went forward on foot. We were darkly dressed and had swords but no armour. If spotted there was just a chance that we would not been seen as part of the army. The enemy were camped in a shallow depression in a large field and a stream ran along the distant margin. I could not see how wide or deep it was, but it seemed to offer an edge to the field. Between them and our camp was a steadily rising hill. If we enticed them to fight I would want them coming up it, I thought. Returning to our camp and pleased about being challenged by our sentries, I called the senior officers and explained what I had seen and what I hoped to happen. I had soldiers dig a chain of knee deep pits across the hilltop just out of sight of the Picts. They were covered with bracken as our camp became fully awake. I dispatched a messenger to find out where our northern contingent was. I wanted them to hold back and avoid being seen.

The sun rose, shining across the fields. The morning dew shone and it created a tranquil and pretty sight. We heard noises of stirring from the enemy camp and I thought it was time to bait them. Our troop now numbered over five hundred, but I trusted in their Roman training and discipline to fight well. I ordered a line of fifty to form at the top of the hill. Standing silently in polished armour, the plumes on the helmets of the three centurions we had in our ranks shifting in the breeze, they made an impressive and forbidding sight. The remainder rested out of sight and protected from detection by the armed horsemen I had posted to fight off any Pictish scouts. I waited for the Picts to notice. To bring them to battle they would have to think they had a chance of victory. To my surprise they were ambling about their camp in what looked like a disorganised fashion. Too much of their alcohol, I wondered. Never take your enemy for granted, I reminded myself. I ordered the visible rank of my soldiers to start beating their swords against their shields. This coordinated action produced as effect as the sound echoed down into the valley. Picts started appearing, lining up, picking up weapons; swords and axes seemed to be the majority. They started yelling, words of hate and resistance. I had heard how much they hated the British, now I could feel it. The leader appeared, breaking through the ranks to the front. He was indeed a fearsome looking man, standing taller than most of his countrymen. He was carrying a great shield and an axe that looked as if it could fell a tree. I thought, and hoped that he would be enraged enough to launch an attack, but to my surprise, the Picts stayed still, shouting and jeering. I realised that they wanted us to descend from the hilltop, to close the two hundred paced between us. We stayed in these positions for about half an hour. A patchy silence fell as people became tired and hoarse from shouting. I had not heard from the messenger sent to the other troop as to where it was or how many were in it so could not rely on that.

I tied a white flag of truce to a broken tree branch, and set off alone down the slope. I stopped half way between our lines and stood waiting. I stood for a few long minutes until Domnall, for I assumed that's who it was, similarly walked forward alone under a flag of truce.

He came to within a swords length of me and asked 'Have you come to surrender? Who are you anyway?'

I smiled my friendliest smile and replied 'You must be Domnall, king of the Picts. I am Carausius, emperor of Britain.'

He looked down on me 'A small man for a grand title, I think. I might have heard of you, somewhere. Aye, have you come to fight us?'

I replied 'You are in my lands and you must leave. It's your choice whether we fight.'

'Well', he said thoughtfully, 'You don't seem to have many soldiers. Maybe you have some more hidden away.'

I tried not to give away any reaction to this and hoped he was not sure.

'I have fine Roman soldiers, the finest in the world. I don't need many to defeat a rabble.'

'We fight then,' he said. He spat on the ground and turned his back on me. As I walked back to my lines, I hoped the Picts still thought that they outnumbered my troops. I was followed by jeers and shouts in some unintelligible tongue.

We formed up again and watched the Picts as Domnall addressed them, trying to fire them up, I thought. Their warriors became restless, milling around and waving their weapons in the air. I addressed my men, telling them they will win because they are the finest, and pointing out the indiscipline evident in the opposing mass. To my relief, they started to stream up the hill towards us. I told my men to wait but prepare an orderly short retreat to where the rest of my troops were concealed behind the hilltop. The holes we had prepared and concealed as traps had been spaced to allow this, and as the Picts reached thirty paces away my men quickly stepped back. To a great shout of triumph, the Picts breasted the rise to see five hundred armoured Roman soldiers waiting for them. Undeterred, they launched themselves forward. As the legs of some fell into the pits, they twisted and fell, but those behind clambered over their bodies to reach us. Domnall was bellowing curses and yelling at his men to keep pushing forward. Axes waved and spears were thrown, but the short swords of my troops thrust and thrust again. Blood spurted from gaping wounds. I saw the helmet of a Roman cleft by an axe. Brain matter and gore pulsed out as the man fell. I swung my sword at the axe-man and slashed his throat open. The battlefield started to smell of the metallic odour of blood, and shit from the slain and wounded added to the horror. The panic of the frightened and the injured started to spread and distract. To maintain discipline, Tertius, my trusted adviser and now firm friend, was pushing forwards towards our front line. I tried to get to him; he was too old and slow despite his years of experience. I had ordered him to stay back as I knew that while he had not lost his courage, his age would tell on his strength and agility. I wiped blood from my eyes and could only watch while a Pict feinted with his spear, then thrust it into Tertius's neck as he flinched. By the time I could get there, he was dying; I saw that this wound could not be survived. I screamed in anger and cut down the Pict. He fell to his knees, dropping his spear and I swung my sword in a vicious chop and severed his head. Domnall's attack was faltering. Despite his superior numbers they were no match for my men. The pile of bodies obstructed the Picts' attempt to withdraw and as a retreat started, I heard a horn blowing and behind them appeared a large group of mounted Romans. My orders to the forts' garrisons had been heeded and obeyed, and the troops had arrived to attack from the north. Such is loyalty and discipline, I thought.

Domnall stared, unbelieving of what was happening, and then flung down his axe. He stood motionless with a group of men around him while those that fled were cut down by my horsemen. The battlefield fell silent. Not even birds could be heard while I surveyed the scene. My men surrounded the surviving Picts and looked at me in expectation. They had lost some friends and fellow soldiers and were itching for revenge.

I told them to wait. I walked to the body of Tertius. My old friend, I thought, why did you not obey me? Why did you think you were still young? I realised that perhaps we all felt the same way in adversity. You did your best I thought, although part of me thought that I had let him down, and that was a hard thought to bear. Having disarmed the remaining Picts we tied them securely. While wondering what to do with them, we collected the bodies of our fallen and built a large funeral pyre.

We returned to our night camp, and I wondered how to reconcile my soldiers' wish to kill all the prisoners and the idea that was forming in my mind. I was the leader: I could not afford to look weak to them, but I had led and fought from the front. I made my decision. While an evening meal was being prepared, I had Domnall brought to me. For the first time he looked unsure as he could read the minds of my soldiers. What he saw was hatred and desire for vengeance. He looked surprised as I had food served for us both. We sat on a log and I stared at the huge painted man, this leader of a major tribe. He stared back without expression. He looked at the meal in front of him, raised his bound hands and an eyebrow. I ordered that his hands be untied and we ate together.

I said 'You are a great leader and I am emperor of

Britain. We can either fight forever or make peace.'

He replied 'This time you have won; you may not next time we meet.'

I said 'I know, but whoever wins there will be death. Do we want to sacrifice our men? I will make a proposal. I will keep my soldiers and people behind the great wall of Emperor Hadrian. I will allow you the lands between the wall of Antoninus to the north to rule in your wisdom and make no attempt to extend my empire and send soldiers to it. In return, you will swear not to cross the wall of Hadrian again.'

While I left Domnall to think on this, I knew that I had no intention of moving my border a hundred miles north to the second wall. This gave Domnall plenty of territory, and I had enough problems to the south of my empire. I was relieved when he agreed. We shook hands in the sight of my men, and we untied his warriors and escorted them north, out of my land.

Chapter 22

Allectus

Society is briefly scandalised by Allectus's blatant disregard of social norms, even though allowance was made for his pagan background. However, Chresima's serene manner and the ease with which she moves into a hostess society soon wins the wives and lovers over as she is admired for her grace and beauty, while the menfolk have other thoughts which remain better unexpressed. Carausius laughed and called him a dark horse when he found out about her. It's a blessing that she and Anwen get on well, as they are both in a strange new set of circumstances. Although an unlikely couple, as a merchant's daughter and a freed slave, Chresima's understanding of Roman society was very helpful to her. The two of them go shopping and a stylish wardrobe following the latest trends was soon forthcoming. The new emperor's wife was introduced into the highest circles of Roman female society.

While Carausius is away in the north, life in London carries on. The routine of my life suits me, and the wheels of empire, now our empire, he remembers, continue to fascinate me. When we are alone, I can tell Chresima of my concerns and she listens quietly, he reflects. We have confidence in Carausius, of course, but I can't ignore the niggling doubts I have about his attitude to risks. Sometimes I feel his optimism is misplaced. She asks why I don't say anything to him, and doesn't understand how difficult I would find it. I worry it would damage our relationship, which because of our differences can be uncomfortable sometimes. It may be my upbringing; the scars in my soul run deep. I have seen the financial might of Rome and he has seen the military might. I know someday we will have to face these.

When Chresima listens to his doubts, she worries about the underlying lack of self-confidence in his nature. She knows he compares himself with his cousin and sees himself as lacking in some way. In a way his insecurities allow her to love him more and bring them closer. Her background as a slave gave her nothing, and now she has everything.

Well, he thinks, my cousin seems to have had some adventures. Carausius has told me of his assessment of the soldiers and his fight with Domnall. He did well with the treaty because it removes the worry of an insecure northern border, I can see that, and I approve of his restructuring of our forces to maximise their effectiveness and reduce expenses. I am less sure of his decision to increase the pay of the rest of them, because that probably wipes out the savings side. I will have to look at that. We are minting more coins than ever but that cannot continue without making them of less value. I can't get Carausius to see that solving a problem this way will cause more later on. Thirty years ago, the treasury told me that a similar problem for emperors arose in Rome itself which culminated in a lot of unrest. Emperor Severus famously said 'Pay the soldiers, damn the rest' when faced with similar problems. I realise that without the confidence of our troops, we will be damned but ignoring the rest is also a recipe for instability. Emperors have fallen for less.

'Things are going well.' announced Carausius, in

summary when our council met.

He had patiently explained his conclusions from his expedition around his empire. He hesitated when he realised what he had said, and added 'apart from the death of our dear friend Tertius.'

He had given the details and explained that he had died a hero's death in what became a victory. I know he carries a great responsibility as emperor, but sometimes I feel he could be more sensitive. His impulsiveness is well-placed in some circumstances, but he needs to remember that a leader has to lead always, and that is s big load to carry. I know he does feel things as a good man does. I see him with his family and when he told me earlier about Tertius, he shed tears. His public face does not define him in my eyes, but he is driven by his instincts to survive and fulfil his new responsibilities.

I stood to speak to the council. I wanted to speak before Carausius rushed in to talk of finding a replacement for Tertius. The rest had just heard, and I thought needed some time to grieve and adjust their thoughts to what was to happen afterwards.

'We need to talk about money' I announced. 'I applaud the way that Carausius has looked at the problems of the army and his actions, but in reducing expenditure one way yet giving a pay rise I fear we are no further on in considering our financial balances. Before our next meeting I will get the treasury to look at the figures. I think income from trading is increasing now that Maximian has realised he needs what we have to sell, but we are incurring great costs with the fortifications and increased number of soldiers we have to hire to garrison them. We know we will be threatened at some point so I see the necessity, but these are costs with no end in sight.'

Carausius said 'Look, I've had some more coins made. Here are some, I can have more minted.'

'You've done what?' I exploded at my cousin. He just grinned in an annoying way. 'You can be so naive; do you think any good can come of this? Valentinus, do you think you can talk any sense into him?'

Carausius laughed. 'They agreed I could be emperor of Britain. That means they recognise me as an equal. If Diocletian and Maximian believe this then how can they possibly be upset by my new coin?'

'Look', I said, 'you made me your minister of finance and I can tell you that we are spending a fortune, money we do not have, in building up our defences because we believe this peace cannot last, and you believe they will smile like you at coins which bear the silhouettes of the three of you with an inscription calling you all brothers? I have not met Maximian and don't want to, but from all I hear he will not take this well. That's not self-promotion, that's a direct challenge.'

'He can't do anything about it, can he? Even if he buzzes around as if he has a chilli up his arse, he has no ships to get at us' responded Carausius, obviously getting annoyed with my reaction.

I said 'You have always advised not to underestimate our enemies. Remember his invasion two years ago. He built his ships away from our eyes, up creeks and rivers. We only found out when his fleet was assembling. That didn't give us much time.'

He replied 'Well, it was enough. The weather did for him mostly and we were ready to take on those we had to.'

'You said at the time we had luck on our side. We can't always just depend on that,' I say in frustration 'I thought you were the great strategist and you think you can call on luck.'

We parted in bad grace. Although we make up later, I had seen something I had not before. I couldn't define it easily but there was an element of arrogance and pride that I didn't like. I had known him all my life, in many circumstances. I had always, almost automatically I thought, looked up to him. I had seen his leadership, his courage and felt the confidence that he inspired in others. For the first time, I felt some misgivings. He was not all-knowing and his knowledge about financial matters bordered on naive. The man everybody looked up to and obeyed without question might be taking us all down a route to destruction.

A couple of years passed quickly and apart from worries over the finances there was little or no instability. I had been forced to demand more in taxes but made it as little as possible having tried to respect peoples' ability to pay. News from the continent was limited. Quintus visited from time to time to speak at our council, but he was uncharacteristically, or perhaps normally for his real nature, rather taciturn. He knew that trouble was brewing and that became clear when some worrying developments started to seep across the channel to our ears.

Chapter 23

Carausius

Addressing my council, I had to inform them of what I was hearing from my lands in Gaul. I have appointed the man who was Tertius's deputy, Probinus, to act as military chief, but he does not have the same experience that dear Tertius was so useful for. He does have an air of competence so I will have to settle for that while I get to know and trust him.

'I am getting mixed and perhaps worrying news from my spies. I am not sure what it means and I will send a message to Decimus to ask him to find out more. It seems that the some of the Frankish tribes who have accepted my position until now and generally not attempted to interfere have started raiding into our lands. At some point we must not tolerate this and will have to respond militarily. This carries the risks of escalating into a bigger and possibly more widespread conflict.'

Probinus replied 'I wonder what else could be behind this. Quintus told me that Maximian is depending more on Constantius, and he could be behind this change in the Franks. He is nearby with a large army and threats or bribes can alter their allegiance.'

The council considered this but came to no conclusions other than it could be something to worry about. I duly dispatched a messenger to Boulogne and spent an anxious few weeks awaiting a reply. When it eventually came, it was not reassuring. Decimus had sent forward scouts to assess the situation, and he said that trouble was stirring. Further south, Constantius had moved two legions across from the east. He was indeed confronting the tribes; those which supported him he sent into our lands to cause havoc and take food supplies. This meant that our peasants were having their homesteads burned and starting to flee northwards. Those that did not support him, he simply started killing until they changed their minds. This was a worrying development. Where would Constantius go from there?

We could only wait. Marcellus returned to Dover and I visited our coastal forts. Everything was in good order, the troops were well-turned out and I could see no reason for concern. It was wise to show my face despite no imminent threat. Things changed when I received a panicking messenger from Boulogne. Constantius had turned north as I feared. He was cutting through my legions with ease. Resistance was strong but my troops were thinly spread trying to defend a wide frontier. Some surrendered but many died, the messenger said. Outflanked and outnumbered, he added. Decimus was preparing for a siege. He wrote that the garrison was strong and they had stored enough food to withstand three months of isolation. Even if the land was cut off, they had the sea. Fishing boats in plentiful waters would add to their supplies, and his ships could travel along the coast. He reminded me that neither Maximian nor Constantius could call on sea power. Nevertheless, leaving the lands would leave Boulogne isolated on a hostile coast. I pondered the situation and realised there was little I could do. We could send ships with supplies and supply more soldiers if necessary. I decided to show my face in a quick visit. I was bored with sitting in offices anyway, I could leave that to Allectus for a while. That was his natural environment. I rode to Dover and told Marcellus to get my nighthawk ready to sail. Darius and my old crew assumed without question that they would be coming along, and of that I was pleased. Such is loyalty. We gathered a full complement of sailors and rowers and half a dozen of Tertius's old marines. I was not anticipating fighting but it was good to have them along. We sailed as soon as we were ready. No stealth was needed, the winds and tides were favourable and we made a speedy crossing. We signalled frantically to the sentries to indicate that we were friends, tied up at the jetty by an outer water gate and were welcomed in. It was good to see Decimus. He had had no notice of our visit and I was pleased to see how organised the great fortress was. He looked worried as we spoke frankly.

'The situation is bad, there's no doubt about that, but it looks as if you can hold out indefinitely. We can re-supply you by sea. We can hope that Constantius gets bored and goes home,' I said with a smile that I didn't quite feel.

Decimus said 'I'm in agreement with that, but being besieged is not good for morale. All these people stuck within these walls with no opportunity to go outside. It's easy for diseases to break out and take hold.'

I acknowledged this concern, and asked about supplies of fresh foods to maintain health, but asked 'Do you think Constantius has siege weapons?'

'There are no reports of sightings of these massive slings and catapults from any one of our sources, so probably not. Or not that could be deployed in the near future. Depending on how the siege goes, things could change later, of course.'

Satisfied that things were as well as they could be, I had my ship prepared for departure and took my farewells of Decimus and his officers. Darius took the ship out and I looked back at the looming bulk of the great castle. How could you even start to attack that, he thought, it would have to fall by siege. Even Roman catapults could not cause enough damage to breach those walls.

Back to Dover, back to London. What a pace of life. I summoned the council and told them of my visit. Not all had heard that I had been across the channel because of the speed of my decision and the need for secrecy. There was some concern expressed that I as emperor was putting myself at risk. I laughed that off saying I wouldn't be much of a leader if I didn't lead. Still the position was that we could only wait. That was not a comfortable position for us to be in, nor one he was used to, thought Allectus. However, when something started to happen it was something we could never have anticipated, and this changed the balance of everything.

A messenger arrived from Decimus.

'I could not believe my eyes. We were expecting an army to turn up at our gates, but they arrived on the other side of the river estuary and made camp'. I must have looked puzzled. The messenger carried on. 'They are not there to fight. There are teams of engineers and soldiers starting to build a wall across the harbour entrance. They are intending to cut us off!'

'How can they do that?' I asked.

'They are moving rocks and earth into the river. Once they get most of the way across we will not longer be able to move ships through. Any ship passing through with be at the mercy of spears and fire arrows. Constantius could even install siege catapults that could reach the fortress. This will affect everything from supplies to fishing.'

'How fast is this happening?' I demanded.

The messenger replied 'I think their progress is slow and will be slower as the river deepens. As I can see it may take several months.'

I thanked him for his information and wondered what to do. I can now see the prospect of the siege succeeding as the garrison starts to starve. Packed in close quarters, I knew that Decimus would be concerned about diseases that can develop and spread like wildfire. How far away were Constantius's troops? Could the garrison and the people get out for fresh air and exercise? How long could they last out? I asked myself. And what in the heavens could I do about it?

He shared this with the council. As usual there was not much in the way of helpful advice.

'We must watch closely' said Allectus, stating the obvious, but adding 'Can we use our smaller boats to keep an eye on this?'

I replied, trying to conceal my frustration 'Yes, that is a good idea. We will have to see what we can do, though?' I turned to Probinus, and said 'You have heard the description and can see the problem. Do you know the fort and harbour at Boulogne?'

'No', he replied 'But I guess you are thinking of some sort of landing to destroy their efforts?'

'Yes', I said, pleased that we were looking at the problem from the same perspective, 'I am going to send you over to have a good look.'

Probinus immediately appeared enthusiastic, for which I was grateful, and recognised a fellow adventurer.

Probinus followed these instructions and Darius took him across the channel. Knowing they couldn't be challenged by sea emboldened Darius and he sailed the ship in so close that they could hear the soldiers shouting and swearing at them. They replied with insults of their own, dodged as a few spears came crashing down onto the deck and Darius made a swift retreat. On return, Probinus travelled to London to report to me.

'That was an adventure. I have never been on such a small ship, but I was impressed by your men. We went so close to this mole, I think it is called, that we even collected a few spears.'

I laughed. 'In the thick of it then. What do you think we could achieve if we attacked it?'

Probinus looked serious. 'To be plain, it is a massive undertaking they are doing. At present it is barely a quarter if the way across so entry to the main harbour is possible. They don't seem to have bothered placing any soldiers or defences there that I could see. We could also land on the mole itself if we could distract or overwhelm the soldiers. Landing could be done, but the bigger question is what could we achieve then?'

'What do you mean?' I asked.

'Suppose we have a significant force of men in possession of the mole. We may have killed some of the soldiers and engineers. We could burn some of the equipment but it is basic and easily replaced. We can't just throw the stones into the river, some of them are massive. I really can't think what we could do in the time we would have before the rest of the army turns up.'

I thanked him for his report and appraisal of the idea of taking the battle to Constantius. Once again, though, I was left at a loss. Over the next few months I received reports of the progress of this construction. As expected it had slowed as the water deepened, further into the river, but in another month or so, the river would be so narrowed that it will be effectively closed to sea traffic. This does not bode well for those inside the fortress, I thought.

Finally I made my decision. I was supported in my plan by a comment that Allectus made pointing out how much money was held in the fortress. The mint at Rouen had been producing coins in my name that were destined for London and held in its vaults. I seized on that as justification for a mission to the fortress but what I really wanted, above all, was to rescue my old friend Decimus. If captured he would suffer a grizzly fate as an ally of mine. I sent a messenger ahead of my arrival to Dover where I followed after rounding up Probinus who was again game for an adventure. For this attack I wanted all three nighthawks fully manned and prepared. This time there will be a fight, I knew.

I timed our departure for an arrival in the dark hours. This time I needed to take and hold the mole if we were to get safely to the fortress. I also needed the assistance of the tides as I was not sure how we would secure the two ships that I had given the task to. We arrived off the coast as planned. The sky was dark and the nighthawks still carried the remains of their blue colours. No lights were showing. Darius crept closer and Probinus readied his troops to clamber onto the mole. The other ship hung back, oars maintaining position until the first ship was secure. No sentries were visible as they approached. The incoming tide carried the boat against the ragged side of the mole. Several oarsmen kept her straight while Probinus crept forwards with a rope. He secured it around a large rock and signalled. They let the ship turn sideways on and the marines climbed silently off. In addition to their swords and shields, they carried spears and amphorae of pitch. As the second ship came in alongside the mole, my ship had reached the jetty under the water gate that we had used before. We had not been able to give any notice of our arrival and again we tried to alert the sentry without provoking an alarm that would set off an uproar. Fortunately, there were two, who recognised the characteristic outlines of the ships and felt secure enough for one to come down and open the gate. Decimus was roused and came to see what was going on.

'We have to accept that with the cutting off of the harbour, the siege, given time, is bound to succeed. I have come to do two things. The first is to empty your treasury. Many coins are stored here, I am told, and I don't want them to fall into enemy hands.' I said.

'Yes, that's true' replied Decimus, 'they were on their way to you. I will get them brought to your ship. But what is going on at the mole?'

As fingers of light started to spread across the sky from the east, the mole was overshadowed by the bulk of the fortress, but as the sun rose, the awakening soldiers of Constantius found the mole was blocked by an imposing shield wall of my men. They had built a barrier with discarded timbers which they had soaked in pitch. The soldiers were unprepared and unarmed, so remained on the land by their encampment. When an officer had been called, he called them to action, and Probinus looked on impassively as a line slowly formed. Because of the narrowness of the mole, the shield wall was only five men wide, but they could not be outflanked.

The enemy commander could not be sure of their intentions, and was hesitant to advance.

'And what is the second thing?' asked Decimus.

I looked him straight in the eye and said 'The second thing is you. We are taking you with us. I need you in Britain.'

'You know I can't leave my men. My reputation and honour are tied to them. You wouldn't either,' he replied quickly.

'The fortress will fall, sooner or later. If you are not here, an easier surrender can be negotiated. You will be executed, I have no doubt. Maximian knows of our friendship from way back. I am making this an order. Come with us.'

Decimus glared at him, and said defiantly 'I am disobeying your order.'

I laughed. 'I thought you would say that!'

I pointedly looked past Decimus who turned to see what I was looking at. I quickly clubbed him on the side of his head, a soldier caught him before he could fall and with another one dragged him down the corridor and steps to the waiting ship.

'Neatly done,' I grunted.

The captain of the guards hand fell to his sword. I raised my hand.

'No' I said, 'think for a moment. Decimus will be treated as a traitor but Constantius is by all accounts a strategist, not a mad dog like Maximian. This fortress will fall, maybe soon, maybe later, but fall it will. When we are gone, make a truce to speak with Constantius. Say you have been betrayed and deserted and only followed Decimus because you were loyal soldiers. Now you can offer him the fort and its harbour with no bloodshed, an army of recruits to serve him and a propaganda victory too. Say you are proud to be Roman soldiers first and foremost. You can even tell him that it takes about twenty years to grow a warrior, so best not to waste any unnecessarily.'

The captain looked hesitant, and I continued 'Look, I am saving your lives, just do this for your men.'

The ships lines were cast off and they started to drift away from the jetty. On the mole, Darius blew a horn signal. The ships were straining now against the outgoing tide, and the lines were pulled in to bring them back against the mole. A flame was struck and the barrier set alight. As it blazed fiercely, the air filled with smoke, and the soldiers retreated swiftly to the ships. A rearguard with spears ready to throw was the final group to embark, but no action was needed. The enemy soldiers just stood helplessly. The lines were slashed and the ships drifted rapidly out of enemy spear range. Soon all three had oars deployed, sails raised and were heading rapidly for home.

Chapter 24

Allectus

After the loss of our lands in Gaul, with our fortress and harbour being the greatest, things were looking bad to me. Carausius was more sanguine, saying that now we had just Britain to worry about things were simpler. He had rescued his friend Decimus and saw this as a success to boost him, but I saw this as a huge price to pay for what we had lost. Leading the expedition himself was in his nature, but I fear his impulsiveness leads him to take risks too readily. He did realise, though, that he needed to reinforce his position to show he was in control as emperor to the whole country. We still had tribes who were, while accepting our rule, ever resentful of it. Some were more likely to start fighting among themselves too, as minor disputes fester and erupt as larger ones. Why they couldn't see the benefits that Rome had given us, and use them, I couldn't understand. We have allowed them to continue so they were still there for them. Then I thought of my father and understood some of this. We also had the northern legions who needed to be supported and kept on side. Carausius rallied us and announced that we were going north to emphasise normality. With our families, servants and various hangers-on, we travelled in a large mass on horseback or in carts and carriages up the great Roman roads that led to the capital city of York. Dressed in our finest uniforms, we were showing our power. For some reason, Quintus and his soldiers came too. I heard him make a comment that he could help defend us in case of trouble, but I knew where his loyalties lay. I felt that Maximian had ordered him to stay close and waste no opportunity in undermining our morale.

Quintus came to the palace where I was waiting for my cousin to join me.

'Well, what do you think of the news from Gaul? Things are starting to happen. Do you think Maximian is starting to get his revenge? Of course it might mean that I can get to go home, so not at all bad for me.'

I looked at him. I said 'Carausius tells me that things are simpler now and that it will be easier just to protect our island. He does not seem particularly worried.'

Quintus stared at me as if I was mad.

'You have lost your lands, your fortress, your harbour and some ships. Do you not see that Maximian now has a strong base on the coast, which you could not take back even if you wanted. The soldiers in Gaul are returning to the command of Rome. Constantius has offered to overlook their betrayal in return for renewed loyalty. He could have ordered executions or a decimation but he wants to use them against you. You are losing control of the great channel once ships are built or brought from elsewhere. His intention to invade is becoming a reality. Carausius is deluded to think otherwise. The end for you is coming and I have suggested that you negotiate your return to the empire until I am blue in the face, but the last chance for that is getting near. Last time Maximian tried and failed, he had to build his fleet up rivers and creeks; now he had the entire port of Boulogne and any suitable bits of coast nearby at his disposal. I am just an old soldier and not a soothsayer but even I can foresee the future on this one. To Maximian, Carausius is a running sore, a boil to be lanced. If he is taken alive he will be given a slow and horrible death. You, who are a part of this, are just a pimple to him and I expect he will just crucify you.'

The thought of this shocks me and I think Quintus must see me go pale as my skin breaks out in a sweat.

'You are the only person close to him who might get him to see sense. You have brains and are wise beyond your years. You understand the ways of Rome. You are almost a Roman too, for heaven's sake. Surely you can see this. You might be able to save yourself and your family.' He hesitated, then carried on, saying quietly 'if Carausius did not hold power then negotiation with someone more reasonable might be possible.'

I saw from the way he was looking that he was appraising me carefully. He then added 'Maximian would be grateful to avoid bloodshed and he could live with a ruler of Britain who served his purposes and ran it well.'

I tried to keep my face from showing any expression. I knew he was speaking the truth and the reality should be staring at us until we couldn't ignore it. There was no-one on the council who could stand up to my cousin. His confidence, his charm and his list of successes all served to bolster his position. He still had the confidence of his soldiers and sailors as he respects them and I have arranged for them to be paid well and regularly. Beyond that, my doubts started. Quintus looked at me. He did not need to say anything. I knew what he was saying.

The door crashed open and Carausius came in. He glanced at Quintus, smiled at me and I saw the fatigue in his face. I had not really noticed it before but he was looking suddenly older. The lines on his face had deepened and there were flecks of grey in his hair and beard. Once he smiled again, some of this was lost and he seemed his usual self.

'I need some wine,' he said, slipping off his armour breast and back plates.

With a sigh he lowered himself down onto an upholstered bench. I poured him a glass of wine, then one for myself and after a brief hesitation, one for Quintus.

Carausius turned to Quintus. 'Well, are you just drinking my wine or preaching doom and gloom?'

He replied 'I was discussing the situation that now exists and the likelihood that Maximian will invade.'

Carausius said 'I think we are secure here. We have control of the channel with our warships, that is our moat. Maximian may have captured a few old hulks but he cannot do anything against my fleet.'

Quintus looked cynically at him. 'Really? You think he will stop at this?'

Carausius glared at him. 'Quintus, I should have you arrested and made hostage.'

Quintus replied 'Yes, you could do that. It would be unwise as I am the official ambassador from Maximian and am your only link for communications. The convention is that I am treated with respect.'

Carausius added 'I can see no good coming out of trying to talk with him, you might as well go home.'

'If only I could, he said, 'if only I could.'

Carausius laughed. 'I told you our fates are linked together. We have been entwined since I was a young man.'

Quintus replied 'That's why I keep trying to talk sense into you. I can't believe you can't see the writing on the wall. How long do you think it will take Maximian to build a fleet? A year or two? He now has the legions in Gaul that you lost. Do you think the men will stay loyal? They will be given a stark choice but they saw their leader run away, didn't they? I bet they weren't shouting 'Hail Carausius' when they realised you had left them cut off and under siege.'

Carausius looked uncomfortable at this challenge, then angry and almost shouted 'It wasn't like that, I had no choice.'

Quintus replied again, calmly 'They are soldiers, you know how they will think. They will sign for Maximian and then with the legions that Constantius brought to the field, they have well over fifteen thousand men to attack your island. Constantius also has his deputy, an attack dog called Asclepiodotus who is by all accounts a vicious but capable military man.'

I was listening to this exchange with deepening concern. I held both men in respect for different reasons, but I could see that Quintus was right. I could see no flaws in what he said, whereas my cousin was floating on a bed of optimism alone. Despite our fortifications along the coast, there were still landing places where bridgeheads could be established. I suddenly thought of Chresima and how good my life had become. All this was at risk.

Carausius told Quintus that he had no more to say and that he should leave. We all stood, and at that point I made my decision. All my resentments rose to the surface. Jealousy, envy and fear surged through my mind. As Carausius turned to say farewell to Quintus, I seized my short gladius sword and plunged it into Carausius's back. I had never stabbed anyone before and it was a strange sensation. Time seemed to slow. A hint of resistance, then an easy passage as the razor sharp blade went through his body. A shade more resistance, then the tip emerged through his chest. He gasped, arched his back and blood poured from his mouth. His eyes locked onto mine in disbelief and he tried to speak. I could not look away.

I said 'You are leading us to disaster and death. I have followed you, worked for you, but you no longer listen. You are blinded to reality by your own mythology.'

I could not wrench my eyes away. 'I'm sorry.'

In his eyes I saw surprise, anger and in his dying moments, finally, I swear, contempt. He fell writhing to the floor and I could not believe how much blood was leaving him as it flowed about my feet.

Quintus stood there like a rock with shock on his face. He shook himself and said 'I did not believe you had that in you.'

I stood there, shocked myself. It had felt unreal, like a dream where I was detached from the world. As Carausius died at my feet, I saw the enormity of what I had just done. What thoughts poured through my mind at that moment. I had killed my cousin. I had killed the one man who might have kept us safe. I had killed the man I looked up to, the man I would have liked to be.

Putting aside these thoughts I looked at Quintus.

'I have done what you wished. Let us talk with Maximian about my position. You are sure he will allow me to rule Britain in his name?'

Quintus gave a snorting laugh of derision.

'You? You think you will rule Britain?'

'But you said.....'

He sneered at me, revealing the hard man beneath.

'Allectus, you are at heart a weak man. I order you to stand down, and hand Britain over to me. Out of our friendship I will intercede with Maximian on your behalf. I think I can get you a quick death.'

I was stunned. Was I so naive that I had killed my cousin for this? He looked at me, awaiting my response. I was still reeling from the shock, but realised how I would be blamed and never forgiven. I would lose my family at home and could never return to Wales. How would Chresima deal with my disgrace. She loves Anwen and the girls and hopes for a child herself. She will lose everything too, and I may lose her because of that. Almost before a conscious thought could enter my head, I realised that I was still holding the gladius, dripping with Carausius's blood. With a grunt I slashed Quintus across the throat. His face showed surprise then horror as his life squirted out in great arterial pulses. There was so much blood on the floor, dark mixing with bright as two lives ended. I dropped the sword and rushed to the door.

Opening it wide, I screamed 'Guards, guards, Quintus has killed Carausius.'

Two burly guards came in quickly and stared in horror.

'I couldn't stop him, I couldn't.' I tried to sob. 'All I could do was kill him afterwards.'

The rest was a blur. People came in and out, gawped at the scene, cried in horror and sadness. There was a sudden commotion outside the door as the guard tried to stop her entering, but Anwen pushed through and stopped abruptly as the looked around and took in the scene.

She burst into tears and wailed like a distressed animal, then as she gathered herself together, she said 'He stabbed him in the back, he called himself a warrior but did not have the courage to fight him like a man.'

She collapsed into my arms and beat at my chest and her tears soaked through my toga. The enormity of what I had done sent shivers through my soul. She tore herself away and left the building. Others comforted me for the loss of my friend and cousin and I was led out into the courtyard. As the day ended, news of the murders were getting around the city. The bodies had been taken away; Anwen wanted Carausius's to return to his family in Wales, and Quintus's was destined for a hole in the ground somewhere. I passed a restless night and awoke to face the planning of what was to happen. I dispatched messengers to recall the council when I returned to London and wondered how I could face them in the light of my guilt. Would they see through me? Did they know that the relationship between us had become more tense? Did they know how Quintus tried to undermine us? Part of me wanted to run back to Wales and hide, but I was in line for retribution should an invasion succeed. I had to stand and fight for my existence.

It was a sad parting for our families a few days later.

Anwen, Chresima and the girls were distraught with grief. Among the tears were mine, but what appeared to be misery was my guilt and conscience playing havoc with my emotions. As she broke down and wept uncontrollably, I moved to take her in my arms to offer her comfort but she pushed me away. How much could she guess? Did she sense the growing distance between Carausius and me? I told myself that she could not possibly have thought that I would betray her husband.

'I will make sure you are looked after.' I said uselessly.

Anwen, the girls, their servants and Carausius's body parted from our sad caravan on the road to London and took the path through Wales to join the great Roman Sarn Helen road to the south and thereby home to Dyfed. I heard later that near the great mountains of north Wales the cart carrying Carausius broke a wheel on the rough tracks and could go no further. In that rocky ground, a shallow grave was fashioned and a cairn of rocks built on it to mark it forever. A humble memorial to a great man, I thought sadly. I hope one day somebody creates a monument of remembrance. I never saw Anwen and her family again.

As we approached London, word of our arrival had spread. People lined the walls and gates, and some shouted greetings, Some even called out 'Hail, Allectus' as if my assumption of the throne was established. A voice in the back of my mind kept saying 'Not as many, not as many' when I compared the numbers and reactions of the people to the arrival of Carausius all those years ago. My first council meeting was a subdued affair. Marcellus, Probinus, Flavius and a few scribes and other officials listened in silence as I described the events of which they had already heard and waited uncomfortably and patiently for someone to speak. Several started to speak together and I realised then that it was assumed that I would take over as emperor. There was an avoidance of emotion as Marcellus and Probinus analysed the military consequences and Maximian's likely reaction.

Probinus spoke first. 'We can expect a renewal of demands to surrender, and even if you are endorsed as emperor the way that Carausius was, it will be because we still have the military advantage. Spies tell us that an invasion fleet is planned, and that is what we must prepare for'.

Valentinus pointed out that we still faced financial pressures. 'I am not a military man but I know that we need money to maintain the garrisons, and I do not need to be told that the forts on the southern shore need bolstering up. Allectus, you need to emphasise your status to the people as well. We must issue coins in your name, with your image and to hold morale in London I suggest starting the building programme on the river banks that give the city its positive direction. We will make economies later, this is too important.'

The meeting ended with the support I had hoped for. In the next few days, as again the horror of my murders kept intruding into my waking and sleeping hours, I was grateful to the heavens that no-one had noticed that in that awful scene full of blood, there was only one sword in the room.

Chapter 25

Maximian

'What in the name of Jupiter is going on in Britain?' shouted Maximian. 'I hear that Carausius is dead, which is good, although I wanted to take my revenge, but it seems that he was murdered by Quintus, which may raise more hostility against us. It would have been better if he had been killed by one of his own. It means that supporters of Carausius are more likely to transfer their allegiance to Allectus, despite his lack of reputation.'

Constantius, fresh from having achieved the surrender of the garrison of Boulogne, and hoping to bask in glory for longer, replied 'I am trying to find out. It will be easier to get spies into Britain now we have more use of the channel. Our fishermen can sail closer to their lands and trade their catches in the smaller towns and villages. Our people can land unnoticed.'

'And what of Allectus? He is weaker, will he now lead? We must find out. If we can replace the ambassador in London we can press again for surrender. Now we have lost Quintus we need a diplomatic mission.' said Maximian. 'In the meantime, appoint someone to build us a naval force for invasion. We need warships as well as troop carriers; we learned that last time. Do this whatever it costs, raise taxes, steal if you must.'

Reports gradually trickled back. Allectus had indeed

assumed the throne as emperor, and Decimus who somehow escaped from Boulogne was now a military adviser. An ambassador was sent under a flag of truce. His ship sailed up the river Thames to London and he had sought a meeting with Allectus. He reported that this was a fruitless mission. Allectus had no trust in any promises of agreements or after that, an offer of clemency.

'He is determined to hold power. The city feels prosperous enough and he is minting coins to support his finances and there is much building work going on. He is showing his confidence through civic projects. It is well fortified too, he's spending money there too, Maximian was told.

He set up a war council with Constantius, Asclepiodotus and his senior military officers. Asclepiodotus was a tough army man who appeared to be fully loyal to Constantius. Maximian as usual looked for any sign of personal ambition that could constitute a threat but decided he was a straightforward capable man who could be trusted to deliver the invasion plans.

'I want an assessment of his strength and a plan to take back Britain,' he demanded.

Planning to recruit more troops and the need for ship building make him consider not just the costs of this and the money he has to raise, but it started him thinking that Allectus was in the same position.

'He has garrisons in the city of London, and the chain

of forts along the coast. He must have more than ten thousand men under arms, but spread all over the country. The loyalty of the Frankish mercenaries can blow in the wind. They need paying and may run in the face of an organised attack. He has the problems I have with a poorer country behind him. He also, by all accounts, has scruples, something that I am not bothered by.'

Constantius laughed, then realised that this was not meant in jest. Maximian stared at him, then smiled.

'Relax, Constantius. Because of your success in Gaul, I have decided to appoint you as my Caesar. I will need a capable deputy. I'm sure we will learn to understand each other.'

Returning to thoughts of war, Maximian said 'We are doing a lot of trade with Britain, aren't we? They are getting money that they need. It is paying for the troops that oppose us.'

Constantius replied 'If we can get what we need elsewhere, then we can certainly stop their money. I wonder how long that difficulty in paying soldiers will take to hit morale? Knowing soldiers, not long. Grumbling goes with the occupation.'

Allectus eventually became aware of this loss of income. Traders complained that they could no longer sell their goods, and grains became damp and perished on quaysides. Imports of wines and oils continued, but prices rose and drained the richer citizens of money.

'This must be hitting them too,' said Valentinus, talking of Maximian's lands, 'he doesn't care, he's just set on retaking Britain. He has time, he is gaining the initiative and has more ways to get money. He could even borrow from Diocletian.'

Sailors and fishermen started to report increased shipbuilding in the ports of Gaul. Larger warships had been brought up from the south and Allectus feared that the invasion plans were advancing rapidly. He knew that his army has been weakened through losses and desertions. Keeping up with the rates of pay he had established was increasingly difficult. He had sent envoys to recruit mercenaries to boost the numbers, with some success with the Frankish tribes of Gaul, but wondered about their ultimate loyalty, and how well they would fight alongside disciplined Roman soldiers.

After a couple of years of stability, there was now unrest growing in Britain. Tribes used to prosperity sent messengers with complaints. Stories grew of soldiers with local roots drifting back to their families and farms. Sensing weakness, more militant tribes started to eye up neighbouring territory. Probinus sent Decimus with loyal troops to deal with dissent and present an image of discipline, and he was away for months. Morale in the council sunk too. The tribal leaders, so loyal for years, attended less often. An air of impending doom started to fall. Allectus minted more coins in an attempt to maintain a picture of affluence but prices continued to rise and even the rich citizens of the capital were starting to complain about the higher prices they were having to pay.

Constantius told Maximian of his plans for the invasion.'We have two objectives; we need to take Dover and control of his fleet, and take the capital which is the seat of his power. We hear that morale in the army is low and that there are desertions from the ranks. I will take my fleet to London, and Asclepiodotus will take Dover. We will ignore the coastal forts once we have a bridgehead. We are each taking a full legion and I doubt that the garrisons of the forts will leave them and march against us'.

Finally, thought Allectus, as news started to arrive. First, a large fleet was spotted assembling in the channel. Reports got muddled, another fleet at Boulogne, or was it the same one. Where will they go? How many ships? How many are carrying soldiers? The weather turned for the worst. Smaller vessels could not sail safely, sightings fell. Marcellus sent reports, and patrolled the channel as much as he could, but his small ships were suddenly confronted with large warships and had to turn away.

Constantius's fleet was the first to make formation and sail away from Boulogne early one morning. Heavily loaded and low in the water, the strengthening easterly wind slowed their progress. Rowers tired and it became impossible to get around the great headland of south-eastern Britain. Some of the ships were forced backwards, others were wary of the shifting sandbanks for which this part of the coast was known, and headed south again. Not like last time, prayed Constantius, let the weather ease. Asclepiodotus had sailed shortly after, against the advice of some of his commanders. Steering for Dover proved impossible and his ships were blown westwards. Here the channel widened and he was relieved to see that the coast of Britain was getting closer despite the conditions. He signalled to his fleet to keep together. The wind finally started to ease, and a sea mist developed. Obscured by this, his fleet made landfall on the mainland near the Isle of Wight. He started to disembark his troops, many of whom were suffering from sea-sickness, and established a camp on the welcome firm dry land. To signal that there was to be no retreat, he ordered that his ships be burned. He has met no resistance. After few days of rest, he rallied his troops, formed them up into battle groups and headed for London.

In London, Allectus did not know what to do. He knew he had no military experience and was dependent on the advice of others. Carausius always said that leaders lead and make decisions, and inspire others to follow. Agonised by indecision he had no-one around to advise him. He knew that he was not regarded by soldiers in the same way as Carausius was. The bonds that military men create when they train and fight together bring a form of trust that he just could not expect.

Decimus was still away in the north, having been sent to raise troops, and Probinus was watching anxiously from the cliffs of Kent. Marcellus was preparing the naval forces for resistance. There were troops on the walls of London as alerts had been called, and many waiting within. Finally, there were trustworthy reports coming in about Constantius's fleet rounding the headland and moving northward, though still at sea. Heading for the great Thames river and thence to London, he thought. Days away, though. Perhaps I should march to meet them? Will Probinus now return with his troops? What if we don't meet up? He is full of self-doubt. I have never been in a battle before, he thought. While he was prevaricating, news arrived of another army, now firmly on British soil, and marching on London from the west. Asclepiodotus, having rested and fed his troops was making good time. In disciplined ranks led by commanders on horseback, they were ready for battle, ready too to restore Britain to the empire and ready for reward.

'This is the real threat now,' Allectus said to his army commander, 'we must march to confront them.'

Glad to have a decision at last, his army left the west gate of London. He was relying on his commander for advice as he knew his troops. He looked around. He was concerned to see they were not a great number, nor did they march with the vigour of a willing army. 'Not as many, not as many,' echoed in his mind. Dismissing this thought, he marched his army on. He did not see, at the rear, a few, then more, men drift away into the edges of the road. Reluctant conscripts, with fields to tend and families to care for, did not like to contemplate a battle against a full battle-trained Roman army. The mercenary troops started to realise that defeat would mean not being paid. It was not really their fight either.

The two armies met in the countryside between the villages that line the straight Roman Road to London from the west. They saw each other in the distance: as they drew closer Allectus saw the might of the forces against him. Plumed officers on horseback, ranks of soldiers on foot, the legion's standard held high, and sun glinting off sharpened weapons. He felt a shiver of fear, and looked round to see his men starting to form up. Both sides shouted a roar of confrontation and hostility. A few hundred yards apart, both armies stopped. At the rear of Allectus's troops, some dropped their weapons, slipped off their armour and melted away into the bushes and across the fields. Shouts of derision came from the other side. Allectus sat silently on his horse in his mud-spattered toga. He looked to his commander for help. The troops in the front rank formed up into a line of shields, ready to fight. 'Advance' shouted the commander. Summoning up courage he did not know he had, Allectus drew his sword and spurred his horse towards the Roman front rank, not knowing who might follow him. Carried away by the occasion, his desperation, his sense of honour and needing his troops to follow him, and seeing no alternative he charged against the Roman line. Against a trained soldier, he stood no chance. While trying to bring his sword down over a shield, a spear pierced his body. He screamed and fell. Helpless on the ground, his writhing form was stabbed, slashed and bled. The few soldiers who followed him were swiftly cut down. Most dropped their weapons, ran or surrendered.

Asclepiodotus dismounted and stood over the body of Allectus. He shrugged, ordered the body to be pulled to the edge of the road where it was left, and mustered his army to carry on to liberate London. He arrived to find that Constantius had entered the city from the east to little resistance, although hundreds of Allectus's deserting mercenary troops had returned to London to loot it. They were quickly dispatched by Constantius's forces and their heads cut off and thrown in a small river. Fortuitously, because of this, some of the civilian population greeted the pair of them as liberators. None was in a rush to admit their support for the uprising.

*   *   *

And so ended the great rebellion. Carausius, a man of and for his time, charismatic and strong, had fallen by betrayal after leading Britain for seven years. After a further three years, Britain was returned to the embrace and control of the Roman empire. Constantius duly returned to Maximian to make his report. He advised Maximian not to inflict great reprisals, to which he agreed as he did not wish to add to his embarrassment and would rather he and history forgot these times. The legions were reformed and brought again into the body of the Roman army. In place of revenge, Maximian planned a great visit to Britain to display his power and celebrate the triumph that he had brought about, and ever one to capitalise on events adopted the name Herculis within his imperial title. To keep Ascepiodotus at arms' length he appointed him as ruler of Britain and left the victory as due to Constantius. Normal political relationships were resumed, administrative structures re-established, and tribal leaders were left nominally in place as before. Most importantly for the Romans, taxes were collected, and trade was resumed to the benefit of both sides. Constantius, who himself was later to become emperor of the Western Roman Empire and start a dynasty of his own line, showed great wisdom and, in wiser and more gracious terms, said advisedly to Maximian 'Oeconomiaest, Stulte'.

And as the dust settled on this event, Anwen and her girls remained in Dyfed where she was treated with respect as an equal member of the royal family. No attempt was made by Maximian to take revenge or give punishment, and Caradog and his remaining sons continued with their business and way of life. Valentinus was allowed to continue in his post and Chresima called on him to ask to be allowed to rejoin the family, and was welcomed, although her status was enhanced, and Marcellus in Dover remained as overall commander of the port. He looked at Darius and his men, who had become such an integral part of his organisation. He wondered how the Roman empire would now treat these brave men that it had treated so cruelly in the past. Using his authority, he solved this by setting up a unit of marine scouts, appointing Darius into his ranks as a commander and putting the men onto the payroll of the official navy. He did advise, however, that they kept their heads down when senior officials were visiting.

And that is the end - or not quite. The Welsh continued to have uncomfortable and complicated relationships with the occupiers. The elder daughter of Carausius and Anwen married Cynan, a son of a half-brother of Caradog named Geraint who became ruler of Brittany. Their son was given the name Ceris and served with distinction in the Roman navy until declaring himself emperor and leading a failed rebellion as Carausius II. His grandson in turn, as the Romans started to withdraw from Britain, was elected by the people as the most suitable leader, also declared himself emperor. He took the name Constantine III and led an army into Gaul in a failed attempt to contend for the remaining western Roman Empire. After the complete withdrawal of the Romans from Britain, tribal factions everywhere struggled for power, but in Wales the ruling families had interbred with Roman aristocracy and later married into another Irish line called the Deisi who settled in Dyfed at the end of the fourth century, and that family line subsequently became rulers of those lands for the next six hundred years.

Author's notes

This is a true story. Well, some of it is. Of course, Wales was not called Wales, and neither was Dyfed called Dyfed; those names came later. For straightforwardness I have utilised them for these third century times. When we consider what is known of Carausius, it is that he was of Menapian origin, and he gained military fame fighting in Gaul. He was then appointed commander of the Roman fleet, with the task of defeating the pirates who raided the shores of Gaul and Britain from the north, and then had his capture for execution ordered by Maximian based on reports that he was keeping the plundered goods. He rebelled in AD286 with widespread support, declared himself emperor of Britain and ruled for seven years until assassinated by his minister of finance, Allectus, of whom very little is recorded in history. The Allectus in this story is therefore my own creation and the relationship between Carausius and Allectus as cousins is derived from the work of Darrell Wolcott, detailed and referenced below. The attempt to besiege Boulogne by building the barrier across the harbour is well documented.

After Maximian's unsuccessful attempt to recapture Britain in AD289, he and co-emperor Diocletian had no alternative but to accept Carausius's rule, while Maximian had to bide his time for revenge to build a greater fleet, finally deposing Allectus in AD296. The coinage issued with Carausius including his silhouette alongside Maximian and Diocletian I can imagine did not go down well.

There are many gaps and questions where history is

silent. The ancient Celtic tribe of the Menapians had their original territory in the Low Countries (modern Holland) and were known as seafarers and traders. Norman Mongan writes that the Menapians settled in Ireland, Wales and the Isle of Man hundreds of years before the times of these events and his exploration of the tribes colonisations have led to the recognition of the origins of many of the clans present in Ireland today. There was then the diaspora from the original lands around 55BC after Julius Caesar's attacks and when severe flooding damaged their homelands. Mongan points out that nowhere in the literature of the time was a place named Menapia mentioned, except in the map of AD150 by the Greek geographer Ptolemy, where Menapia is firmly situated on the east coast of Ireland where Wexford is today. The reference to the origin of Carausius by Aurelius Victor, a Roman historian writing in the fourth century, was as 'Menapian', *(Quo bello Carausius Menapiae civis)*. This has been repeatedly interpreted by historians as implying a direct origin from the Low Countries, whereas as Mongan points out, the text does not say *Menapius civis*. This important distinction widens the debate over the historical origins of this family line to include the many other Menapian settlements in Ireland, particularly the ones at Wexford, and west Wales which were simply referred to later as Menapia too. The work of Darrell Wolcott, see below, identifies the family line that probably came to Wales via Ireland.

There are two inscriptions in stone of the name Carausius, a rare name that appears nowhere in Europe. The first is on a milestone near Carlisle, and the second is now in the church in the village of Penmachno, on the southern edge of Snowdonia in north Wales. On it is the inscription *'Here lies Carausius under this pile of stones'*. This dates from the fifth century and bears a Christian symbol and on this basis it has been disassociated from this rebellion. In view of the fact that descendents of his extended family still ruled Wales, and had most likely adopted Christianity, it would be nice, and not inconceivable, to conjecture that our Carausius's memory was later preserved and respected by his family after his death.

History is also silent about why a soldier was given command of the Roman navy? Why did Carausius have so much support in Britain and northern Gaul when he rebelled? Why did Allectus kill him? Why did not Allectus surrender to Maximian?

This story fascinated me when I discovered it after researching my wife's family history and her descent through another half-brother of Caradog, Eudaf. Through this I have acquired many of what I call my historical pen-friends. The extensive work of Darrell Wolcott and in particular his papers on the Royal Roman family of Britain and the pedigrees of Llyr Llediarth's descendents provided the skeleton and links, and the books of two people, (unbeknown to them) allowed me to create the story. Stuart Laycock, who with Miles Russell wrote *UnRoman Britain* provided the arguments about the benefits of Romanisation to the rulers in Britain and the taking of rulers' children into military service or to be educated in Roman ways. Sam Moorhead in his book with David Stuttard *The Romans who shaped Britain* drew a beautiful vignette of Carausius capturing a pirate ship that then captured my imagination. Special thanks are due to Dr Benet Salway of University College London, who as an academic historian has patiently tried to keep my story as accurate as possible, 'to turn fantasy into historical fiction', as he put it. Apologies to him for ignoring a few of his points; I had to over-ride some to maintain the flow of the story!

This story has been told in fiction twice in the last century. Rosemary Sutcliff wrote the childrens' story *'The Silver Branch'* in 1957, and John Gloag wrote *'The Caesar of the Narrow Sea'*, in 1969. It is well worth re-visiting and I am happy to offer my interpretation here.

I can imagine some historians circling like vultures to pick holes in my story. Is this history or just a tale? What I offer here is I believe a plausible version of the overall Carausius and Allectus story that uses both the known history and the published opinions of many others to address the questions and fill the gaps with events and circumstances current at the time. I hope you have enjoyed it; all the faults are mine, of course.

A chronologically stable pedigree

(after Darrell Wolcott)

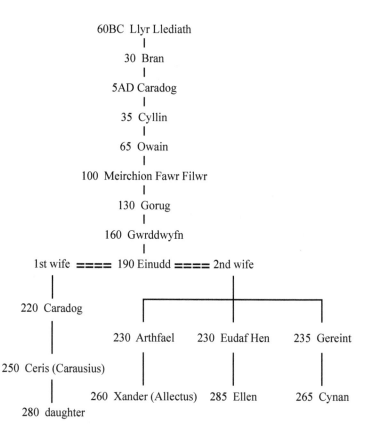

Further reading

Casey PJ. *Carausius and Allectus*. Yale University Press, New Haven and London, 1994.

Laycock S, Russell M. *UnRoman Britain*. The History Press, Cheltenham 2010.

Merroney M. *Some thoughts on the Romanisation of Pembrokeshire*. Pembrokeshire Historical Society. https://www.pembrokeshirehistoricalsociety.co.uk/thoughts-romanisation-pembrokeshire 2018.

Mongan N. *The Menapia Quest.* The Herodotus Press, Dublin, 1995.

Moorhead S, Stuttard D. *The Romans who shaped Britain.* Thames and Hudson, London 2012.

Wolcott D. Center for the Study of Ancient Wales, Jefferson, Texas, USA. *Britain's Royal Roman Family* and *Beli Mawr and Llyr Llediarth in Welsh pedigrees.*
www.ancientwalesstudies.org

For more information see www.carausius.org

The Author

John Pitts is a retired family doctor and medical educationalist who practised near Southampton. Brought up in Cardiff, he has moved back and recently married his childhood sweetheart. Exploring her family history led back further and further in time and this little-known episode in British history emerged.

Ingram Content Group UK Ltd.
Milton Keynes UK
UKHW011437060323
418105UK00019B/2085